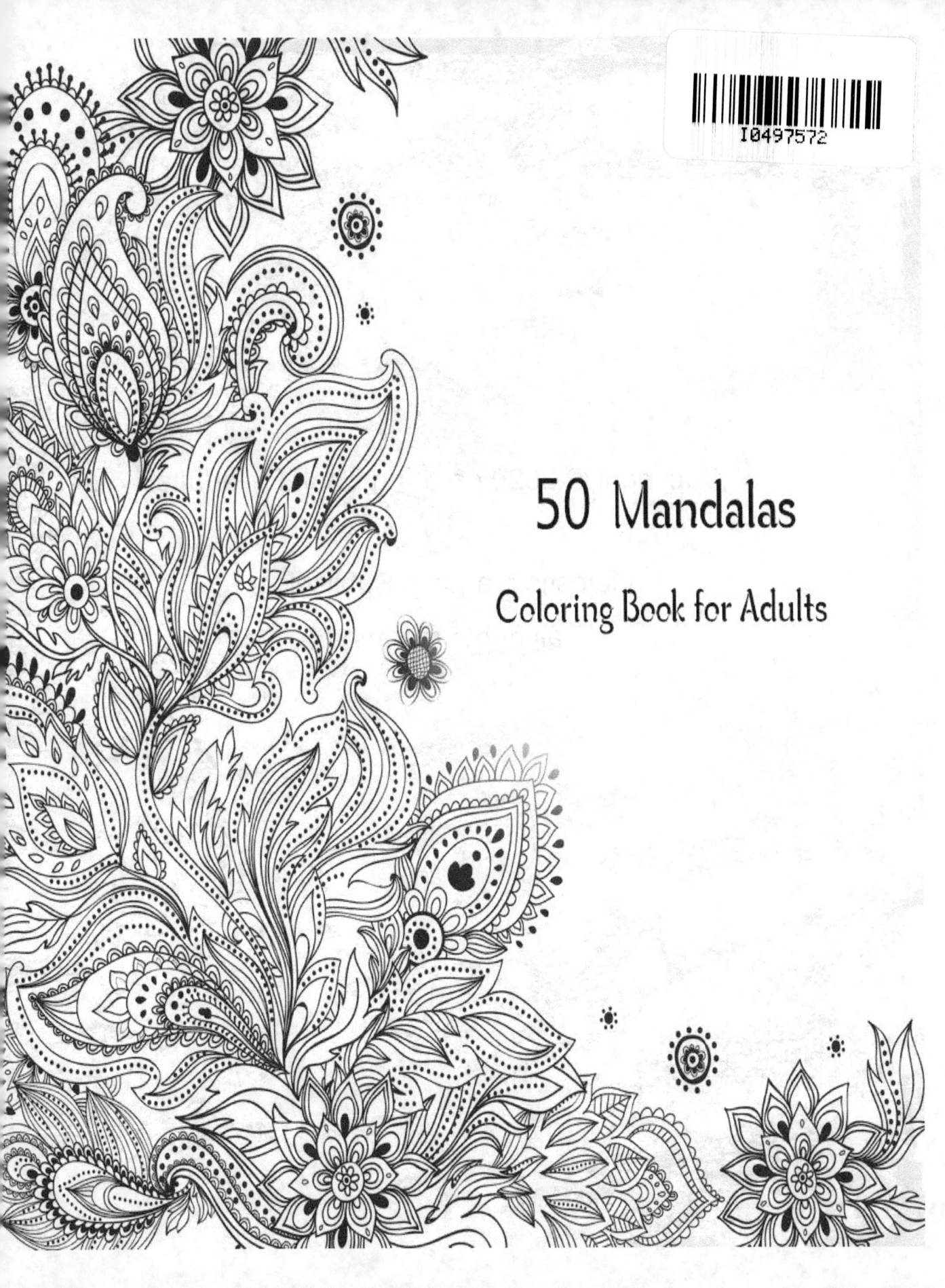

# 50 Mandalas

Coloring Book for Adults

Copyright © 2020, coloring book for adults

by

Majestic Mandala Publishing

all rights reserved.

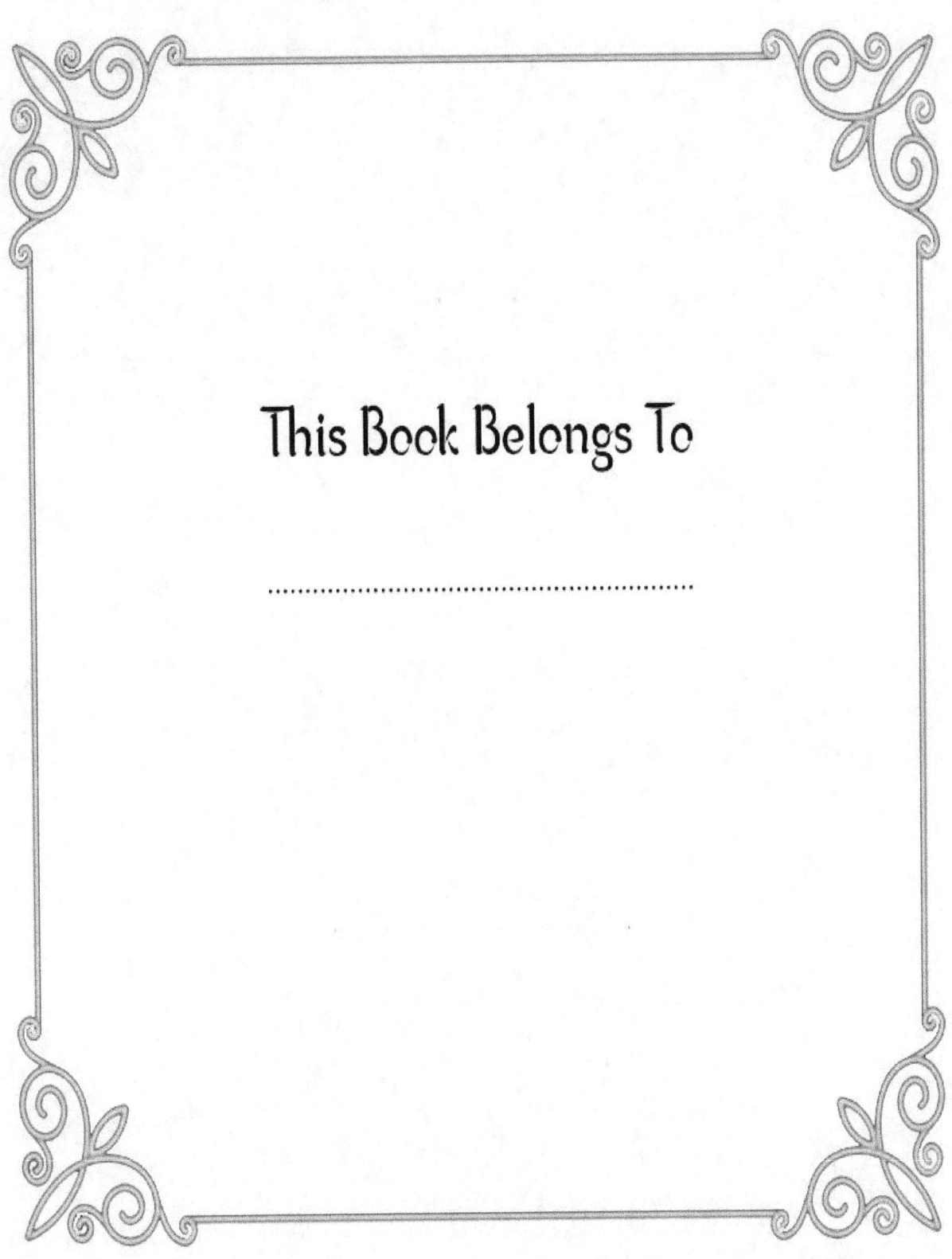

# This Book Belongs To

..................................................

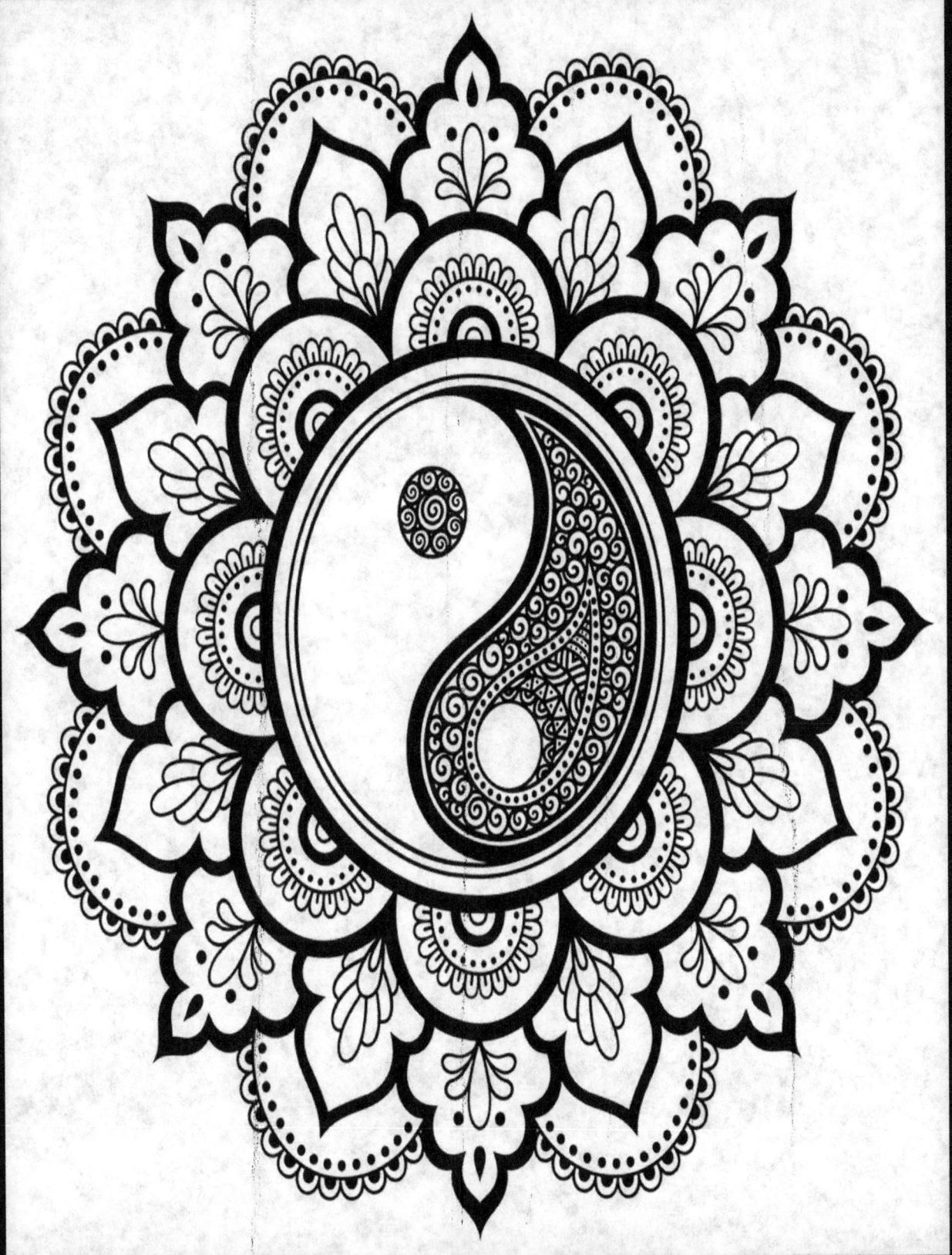

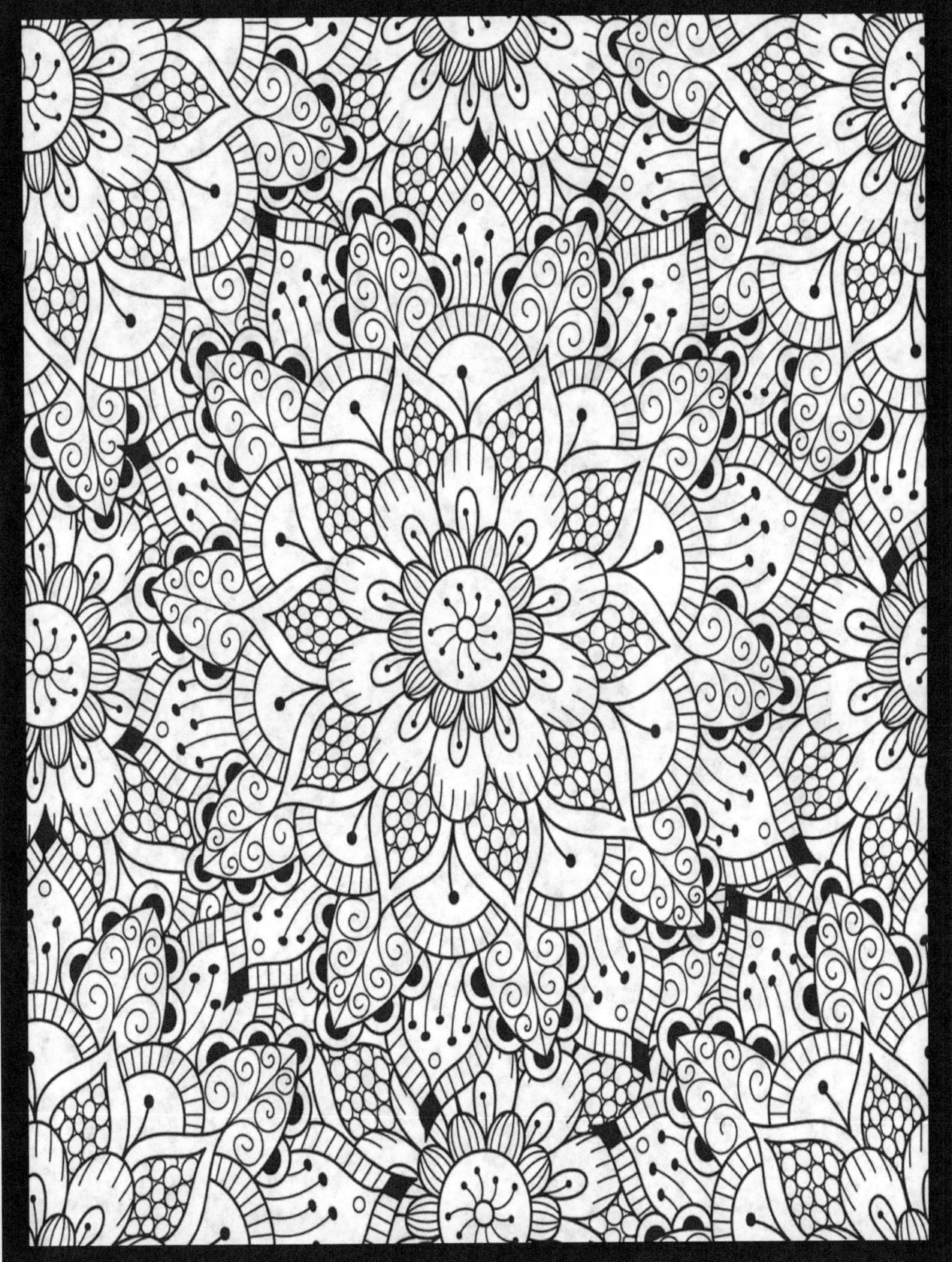

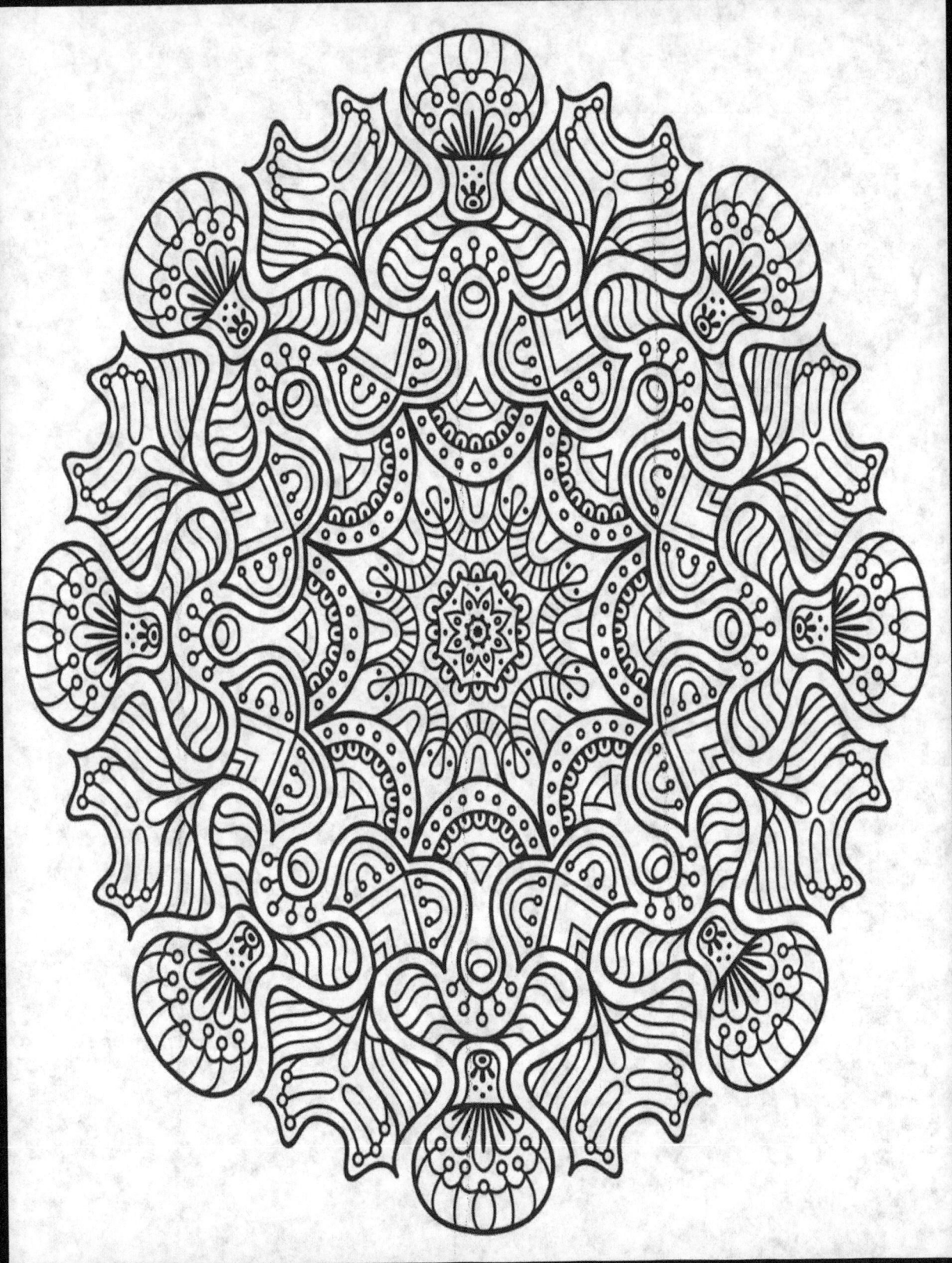

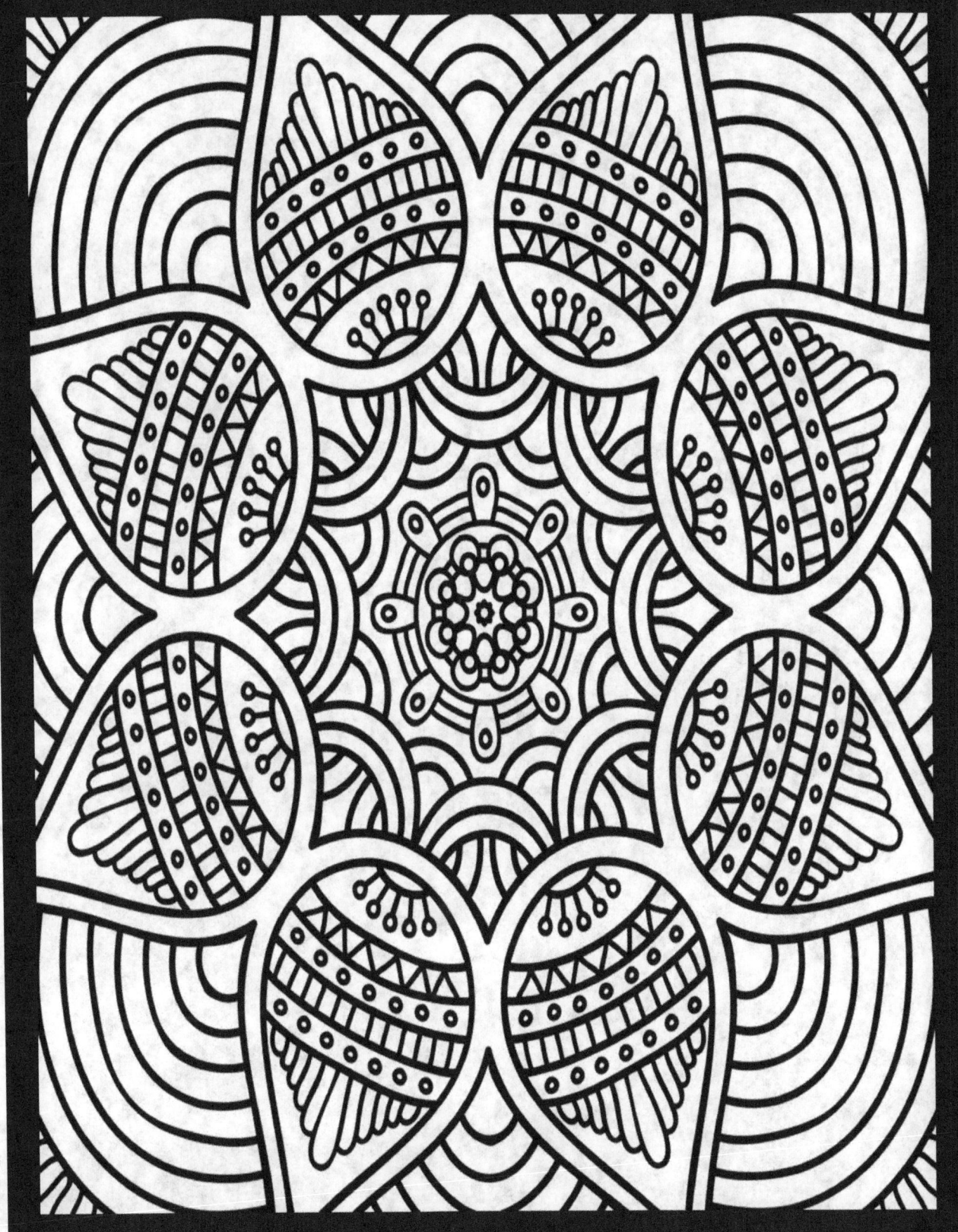

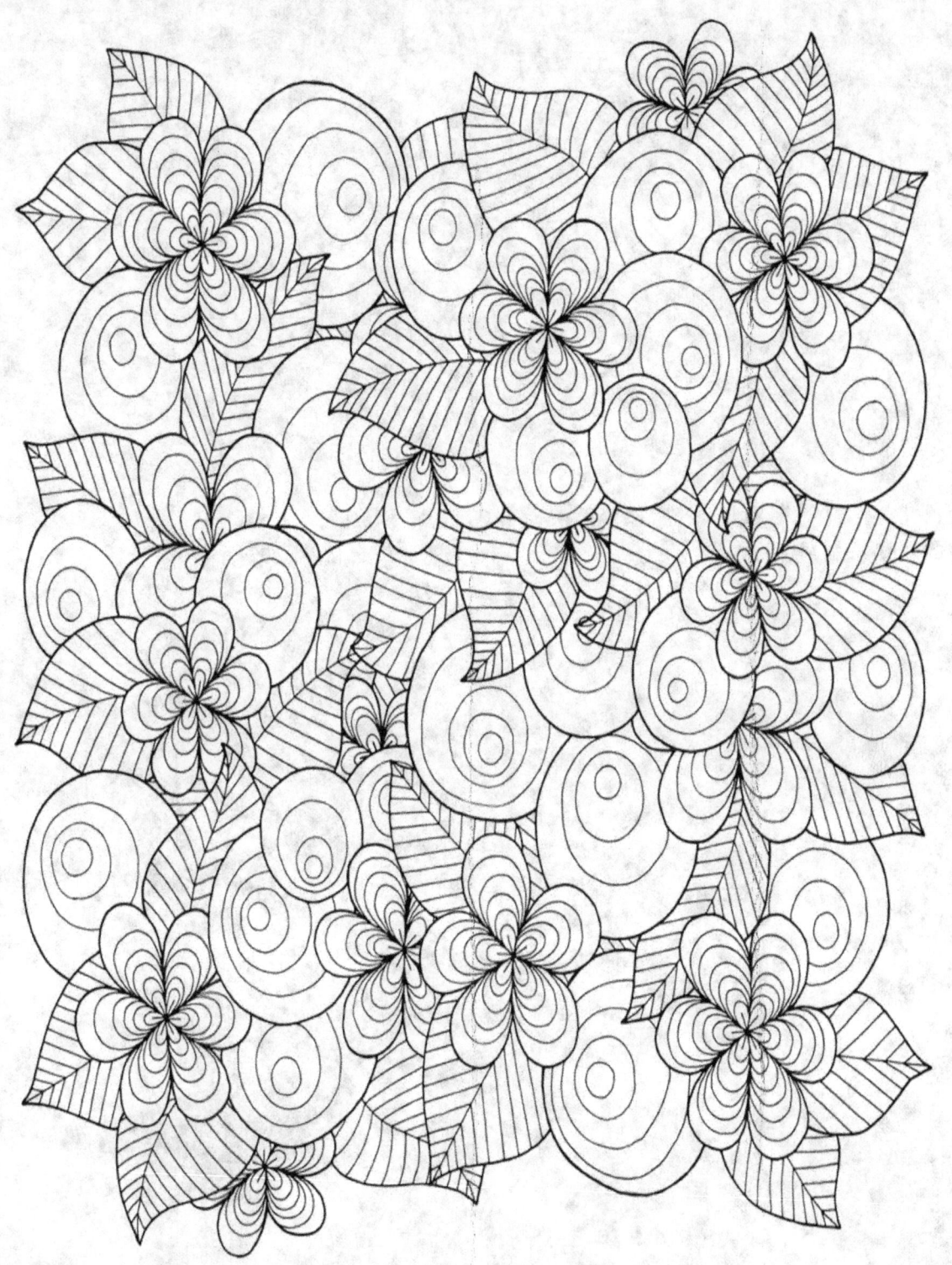

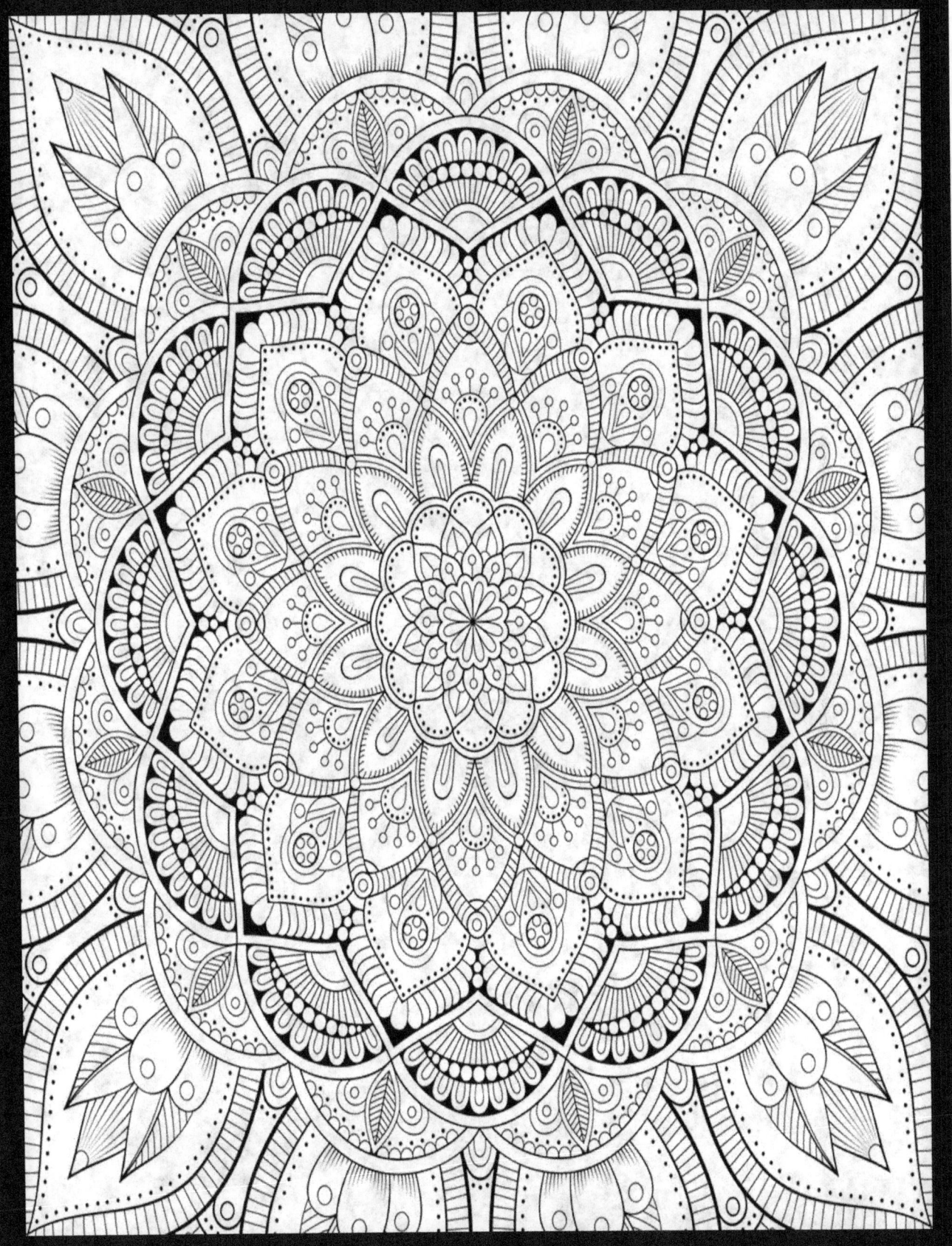

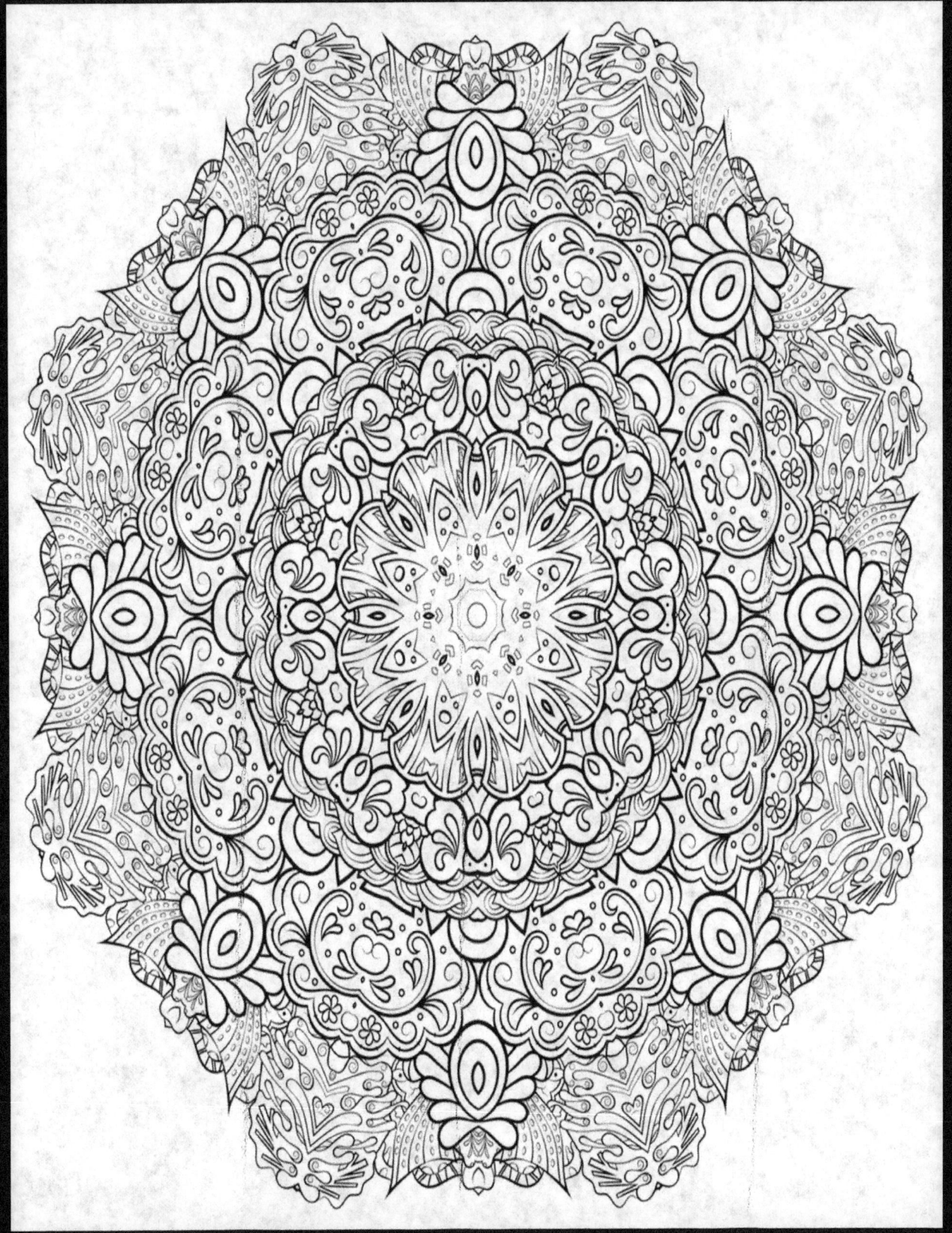

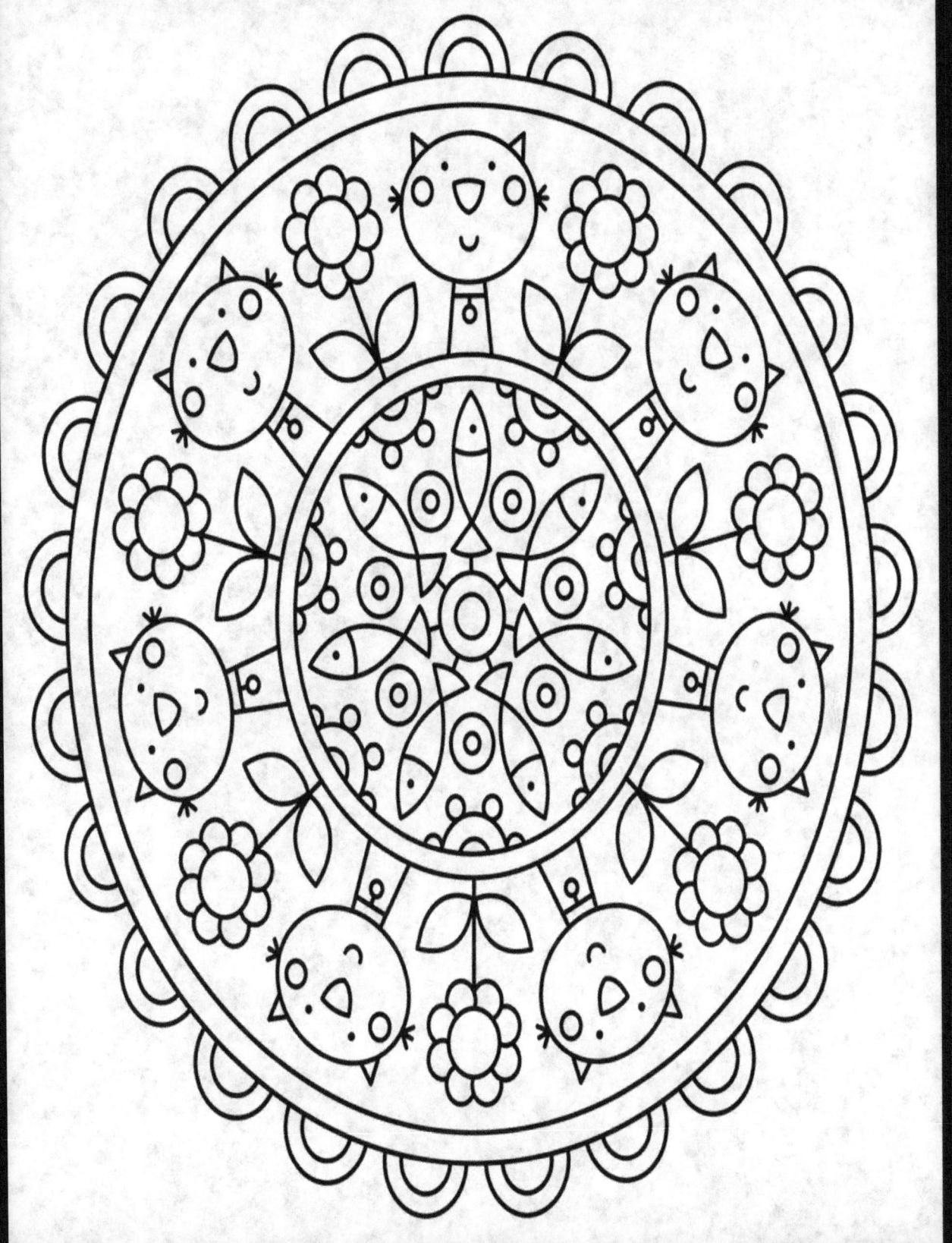

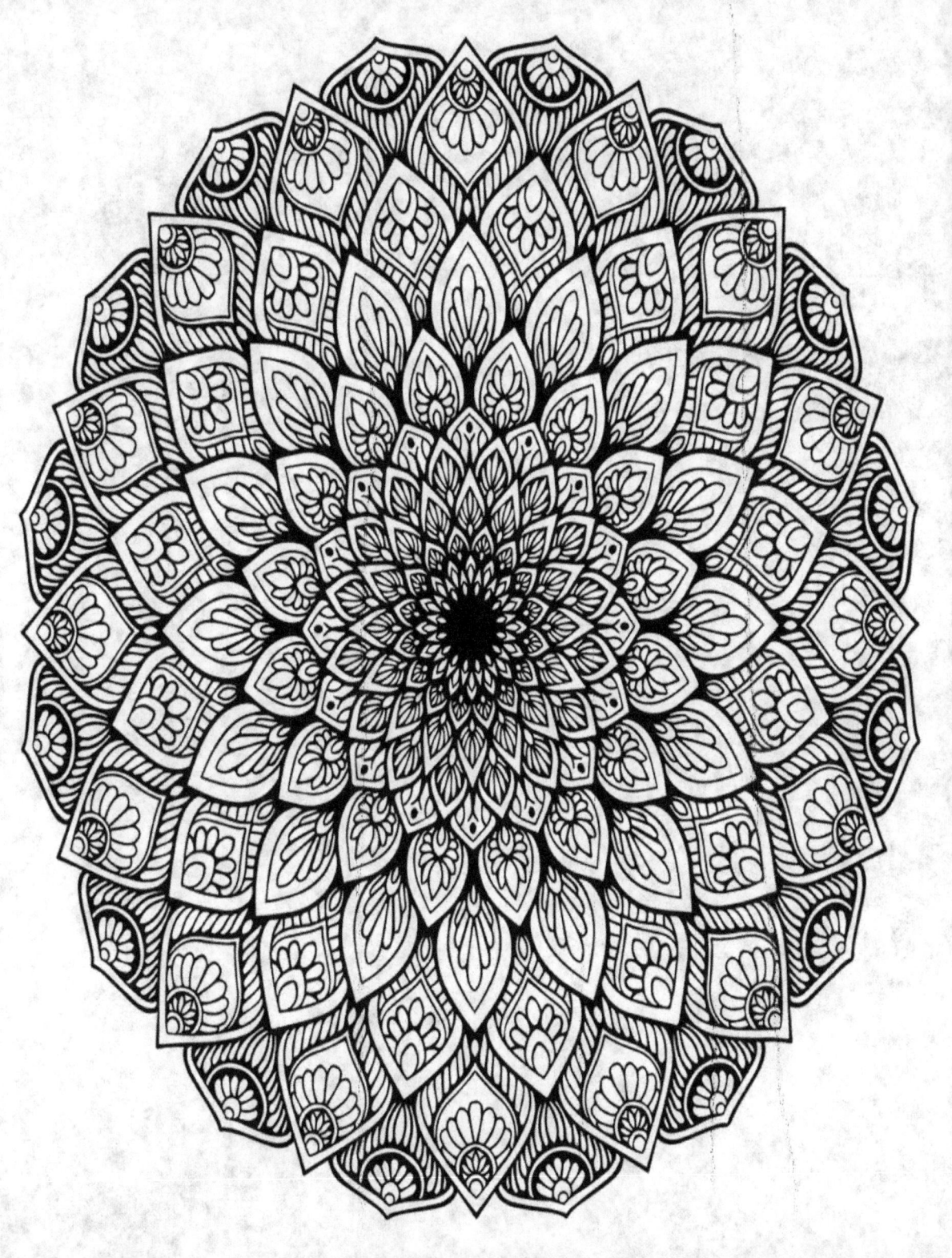

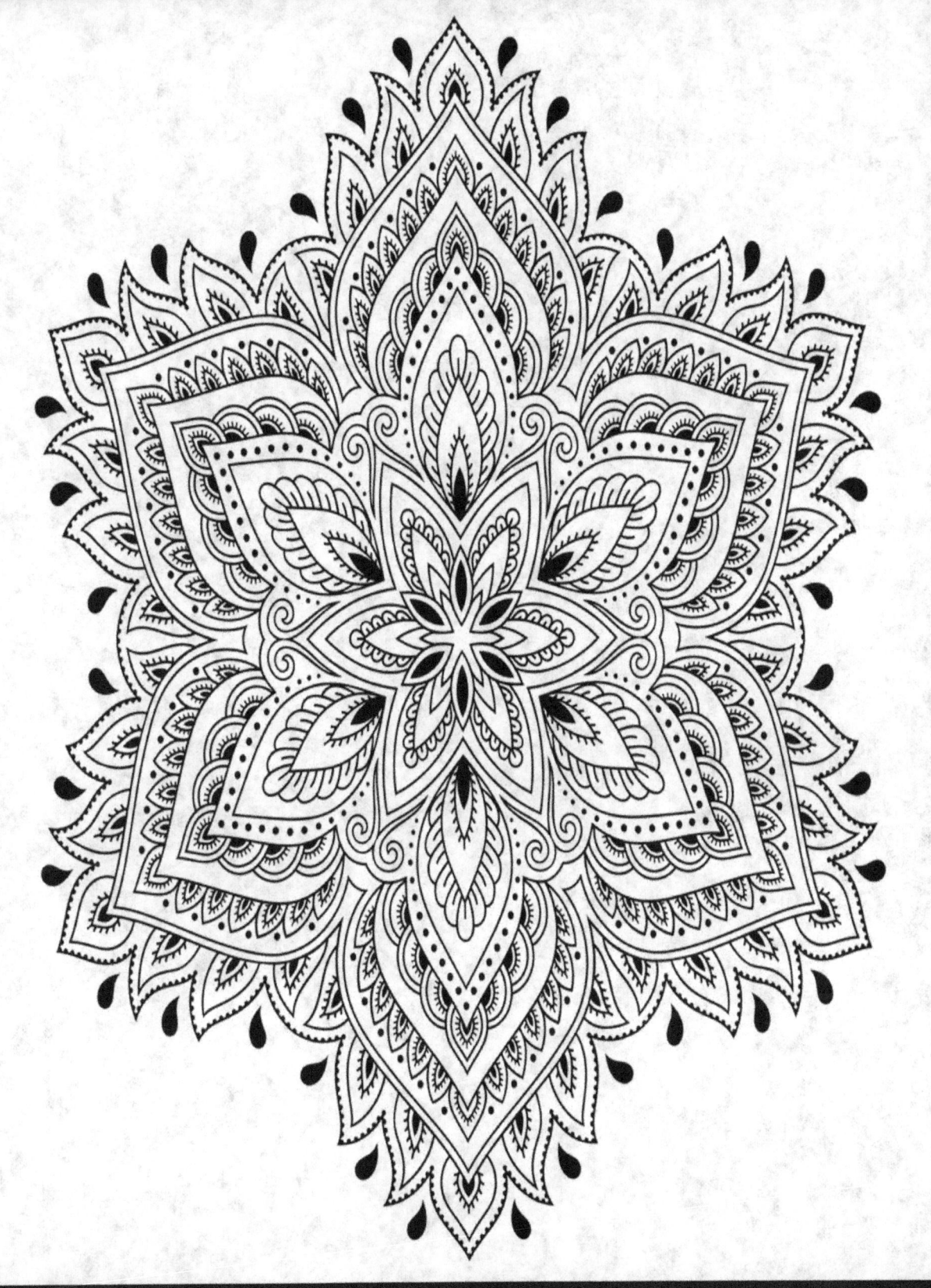

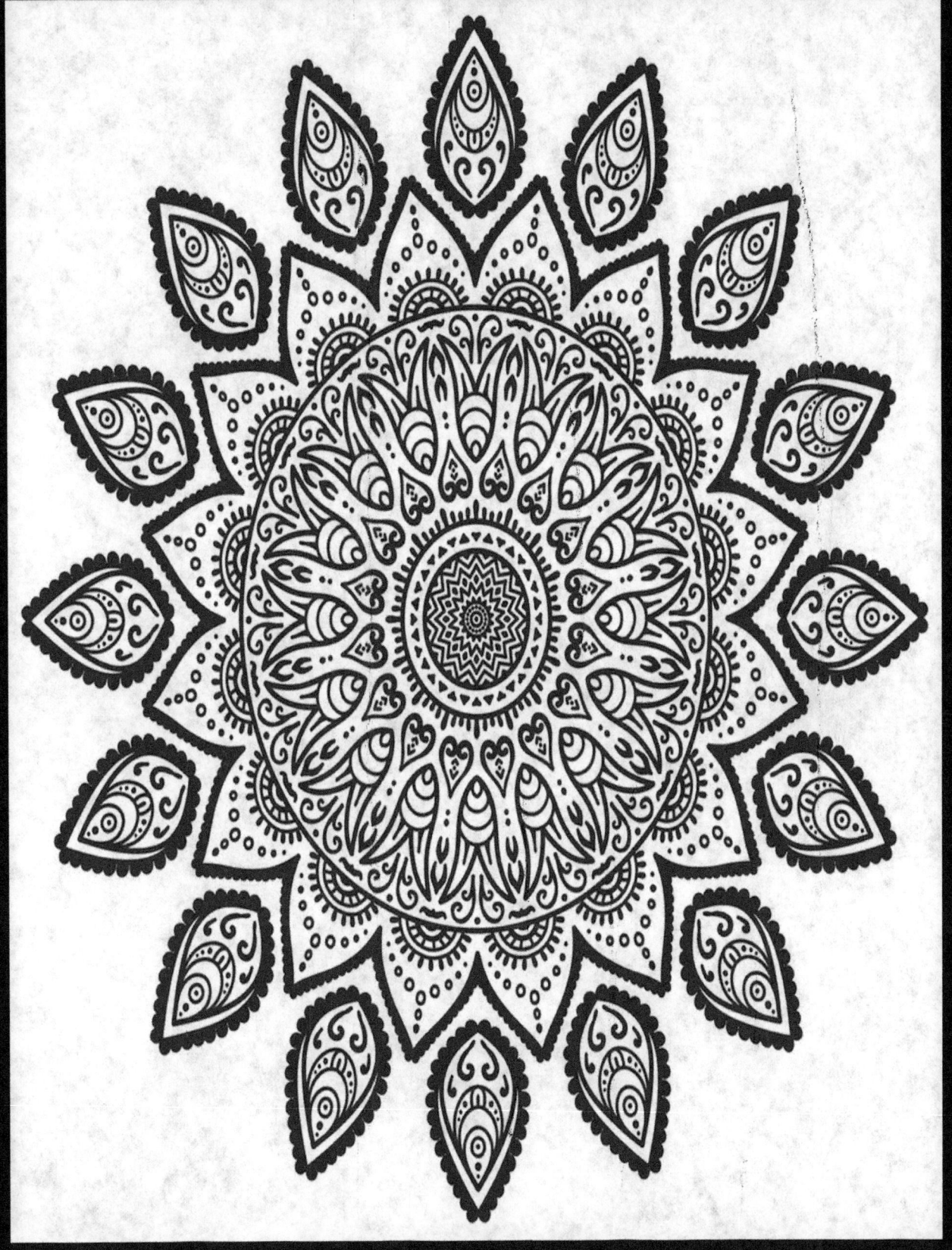

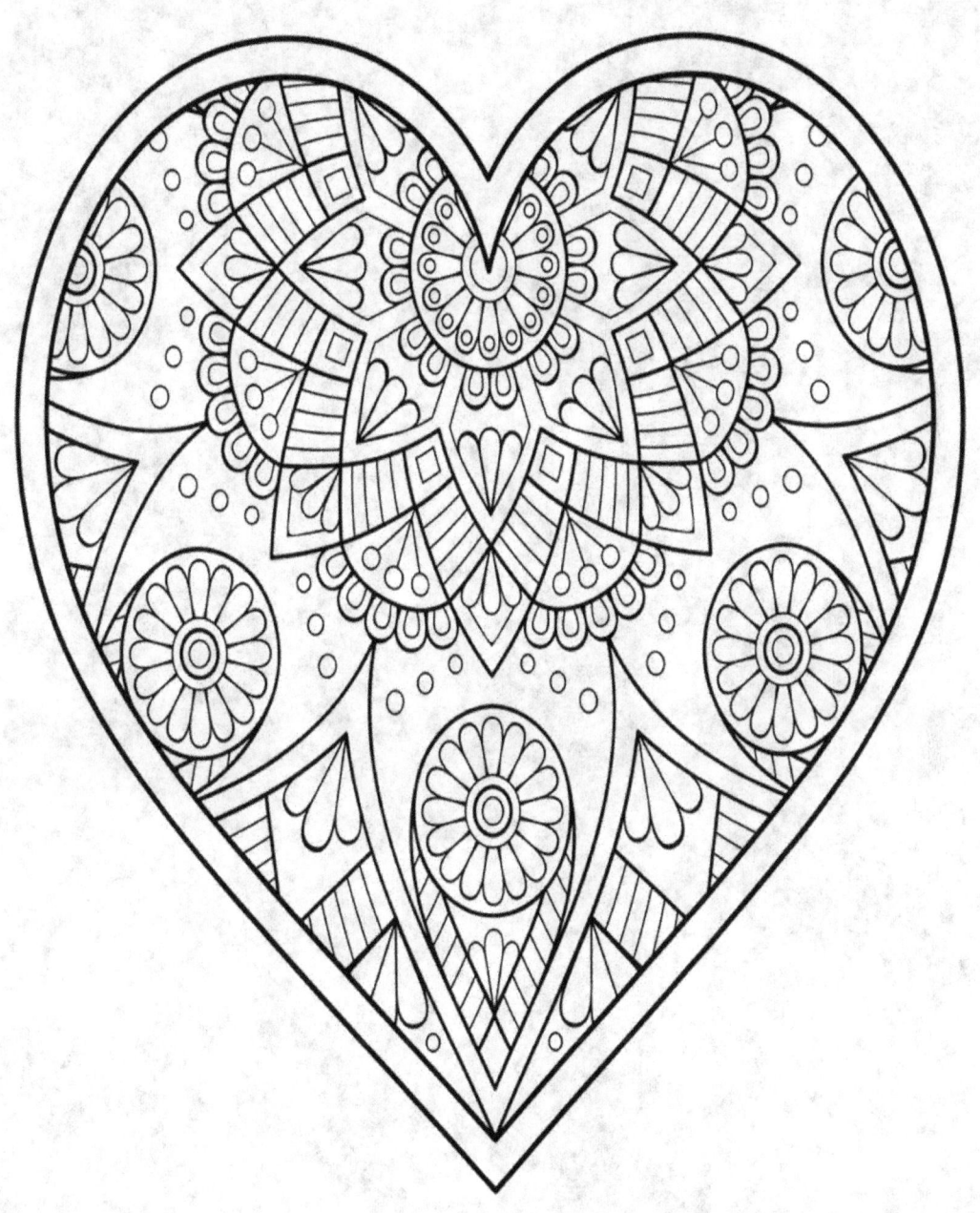

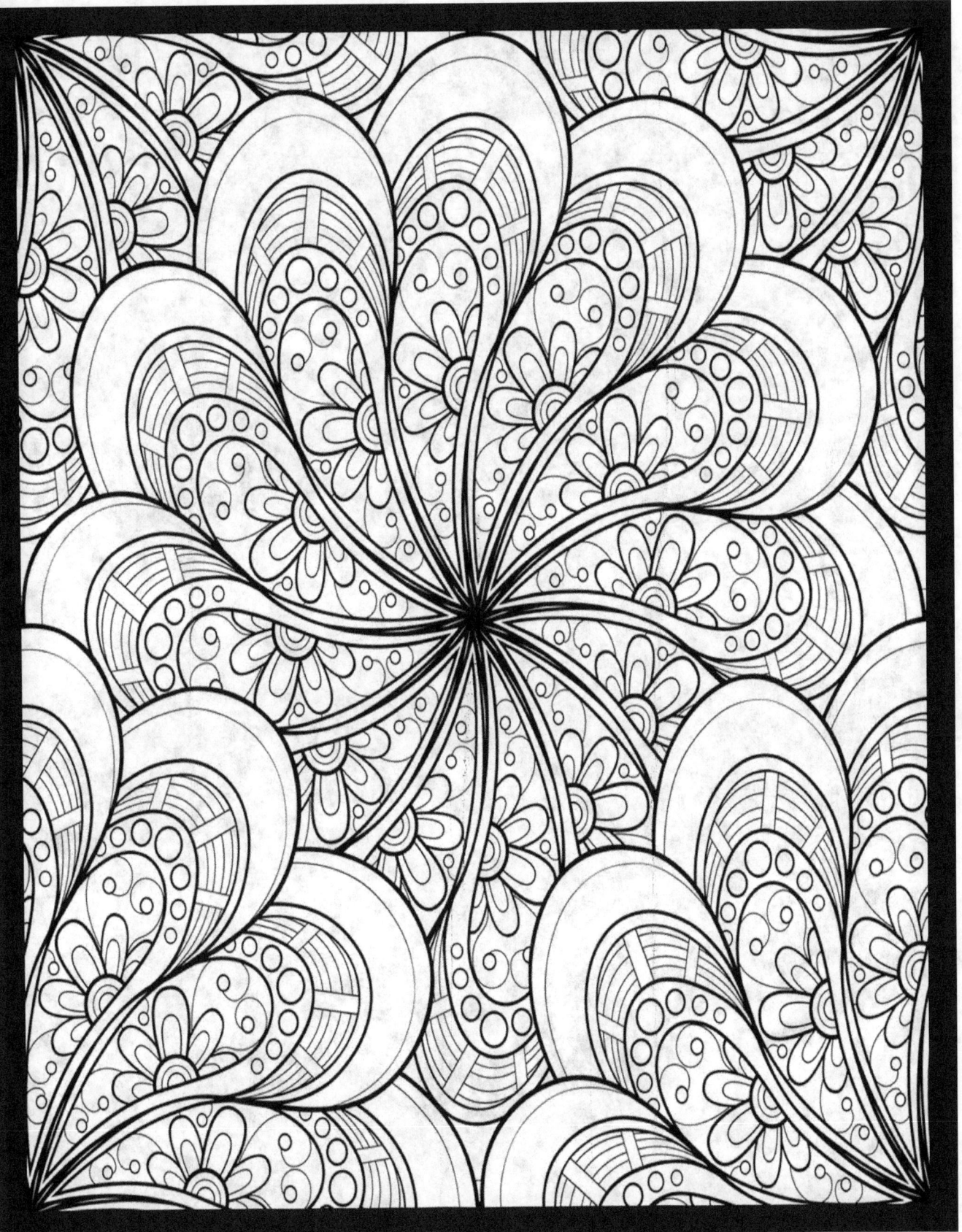

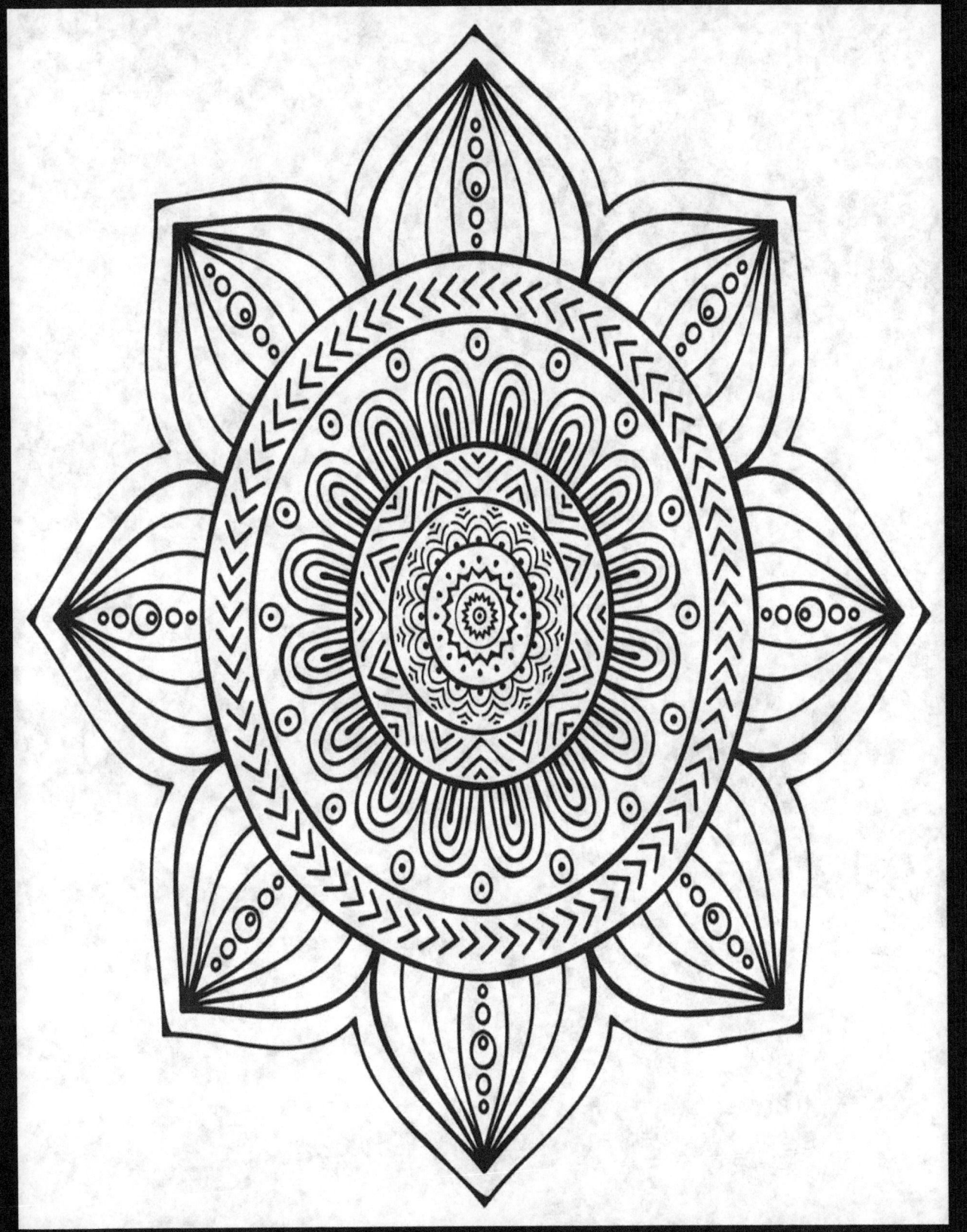

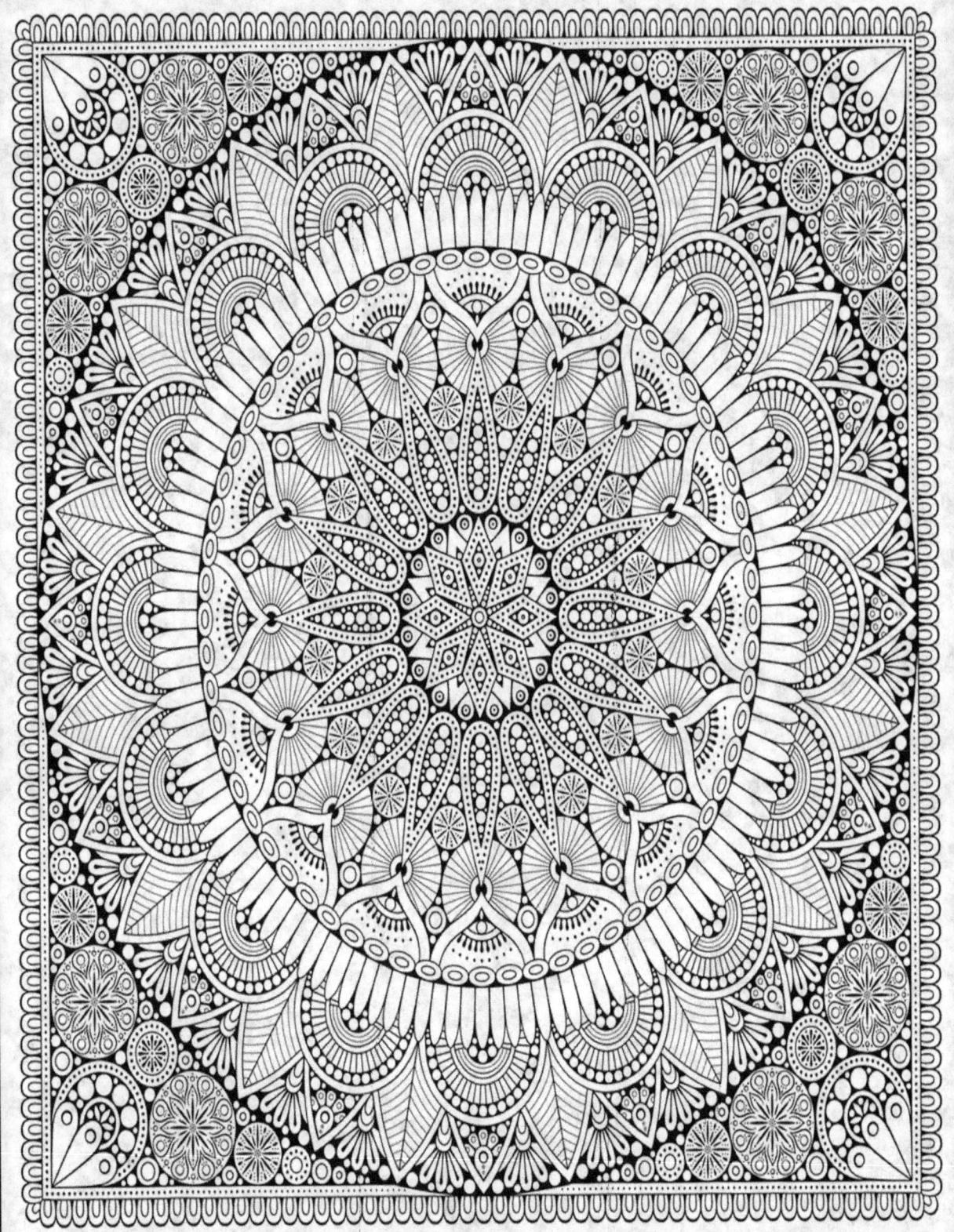

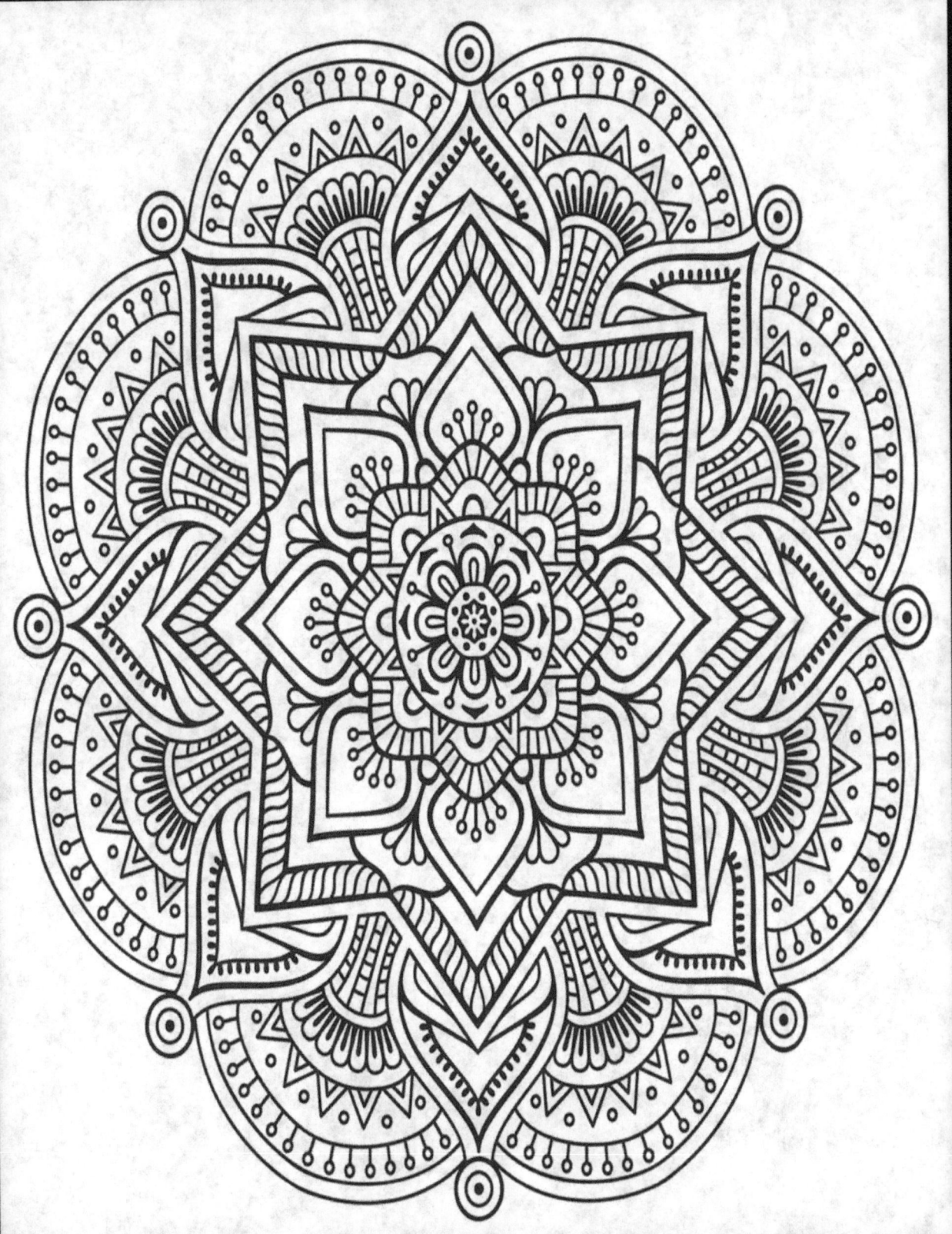

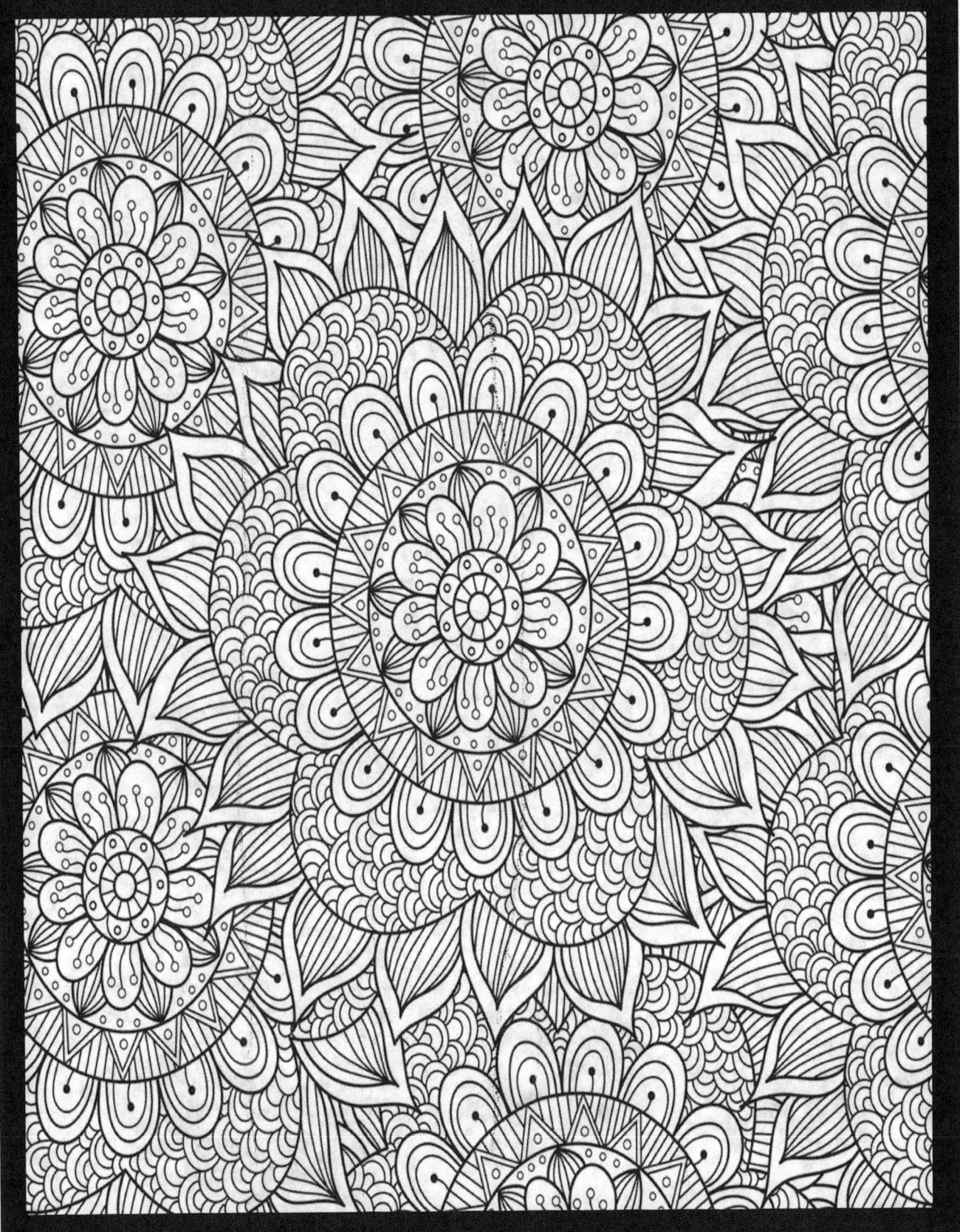

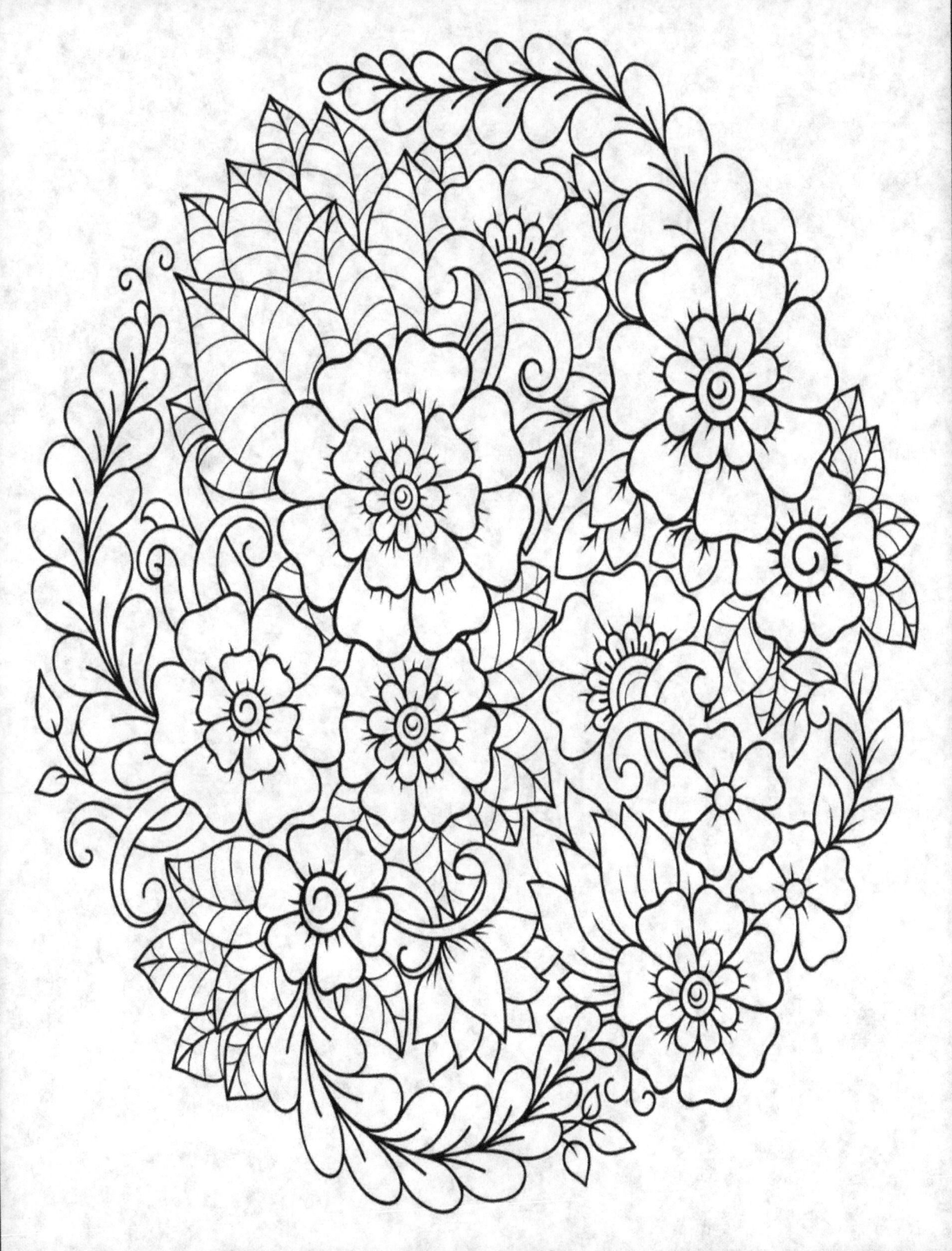

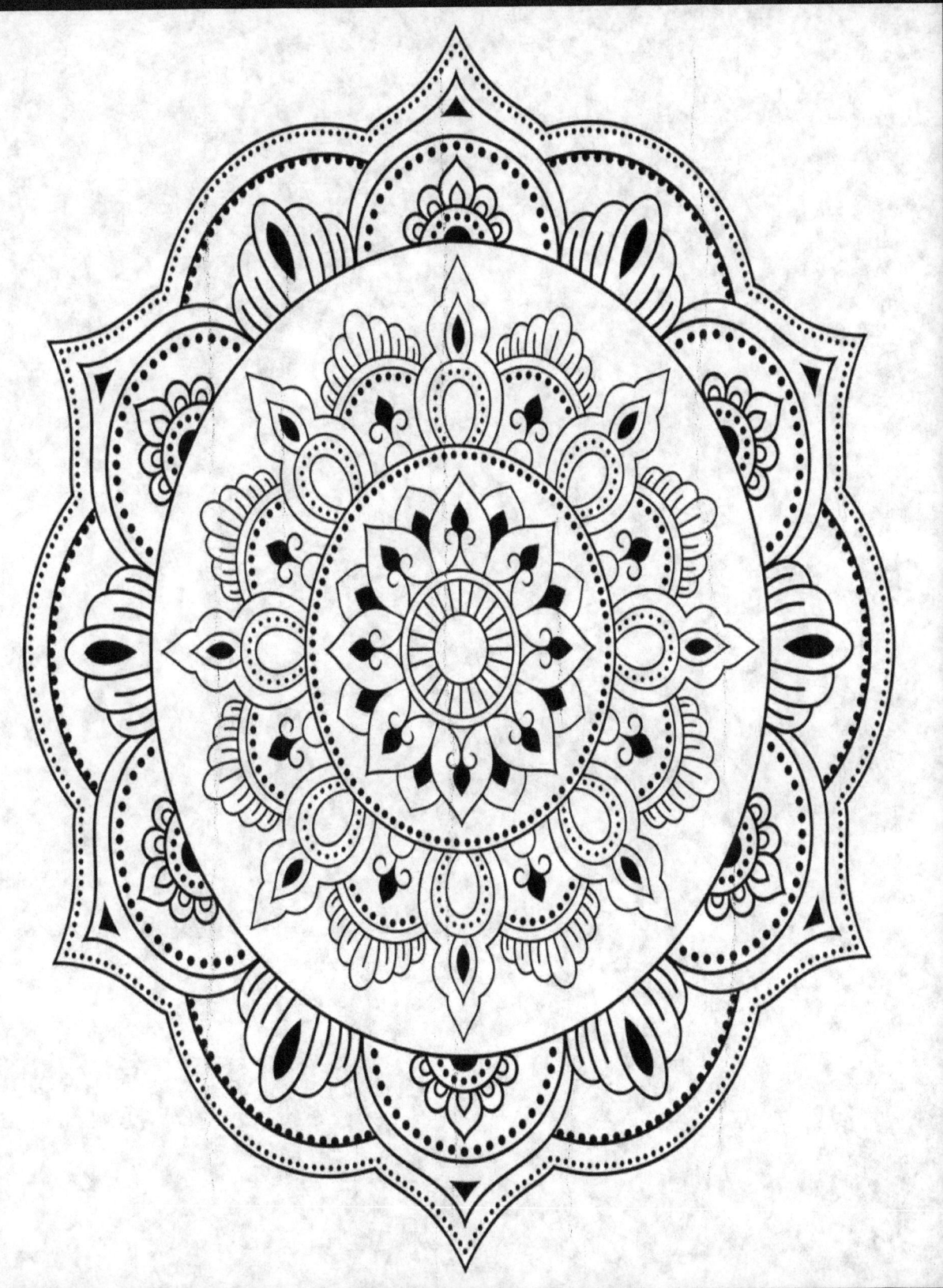

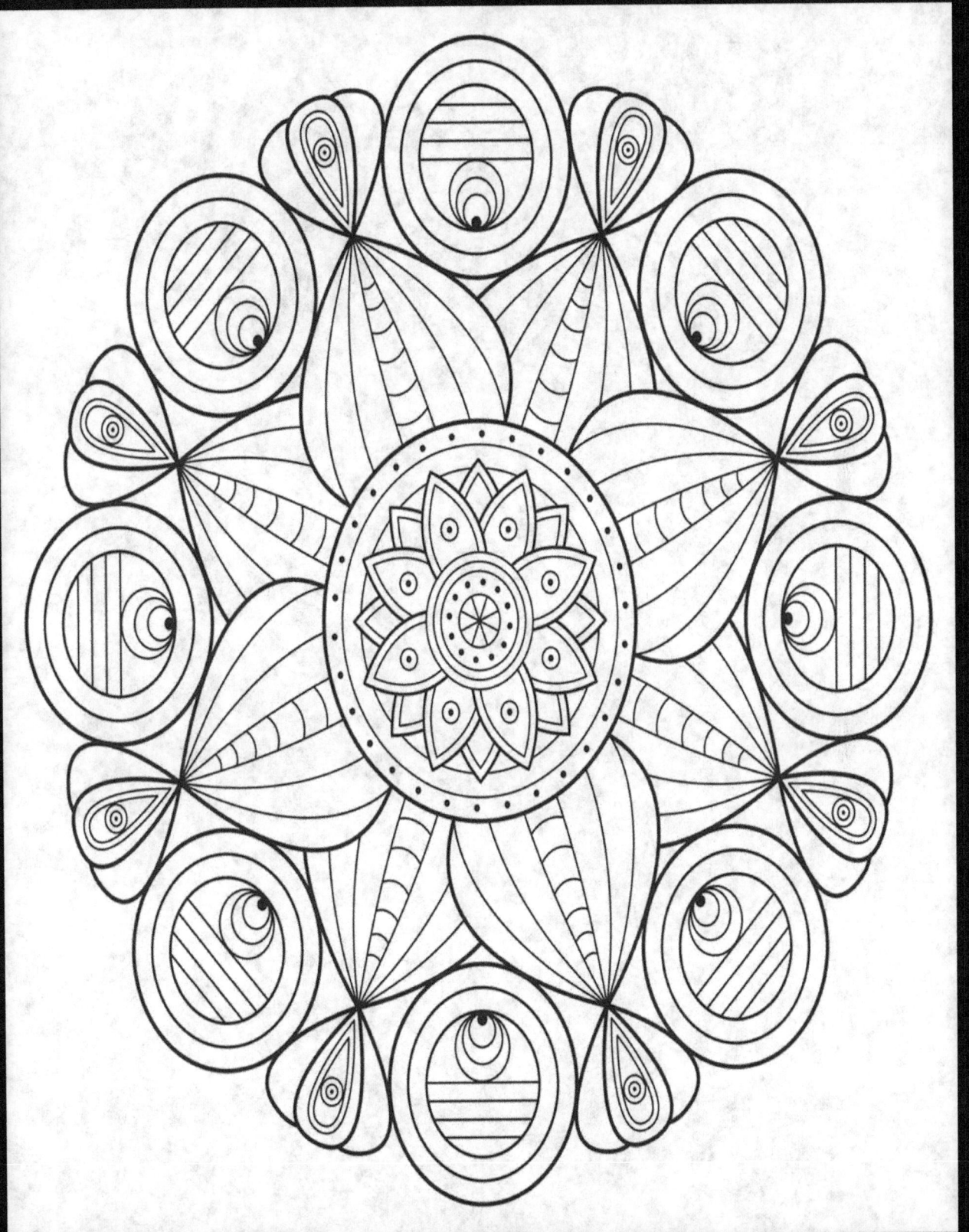

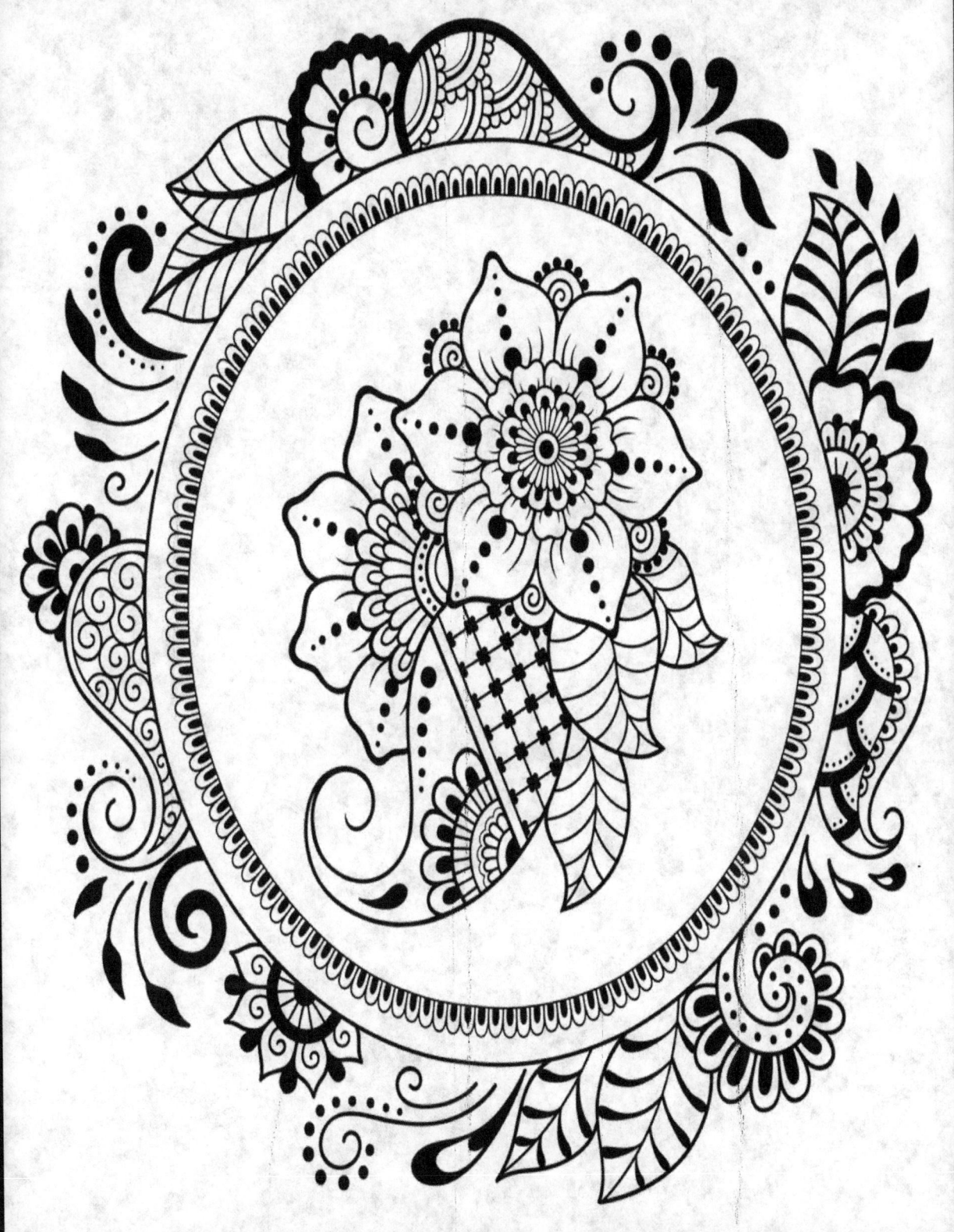

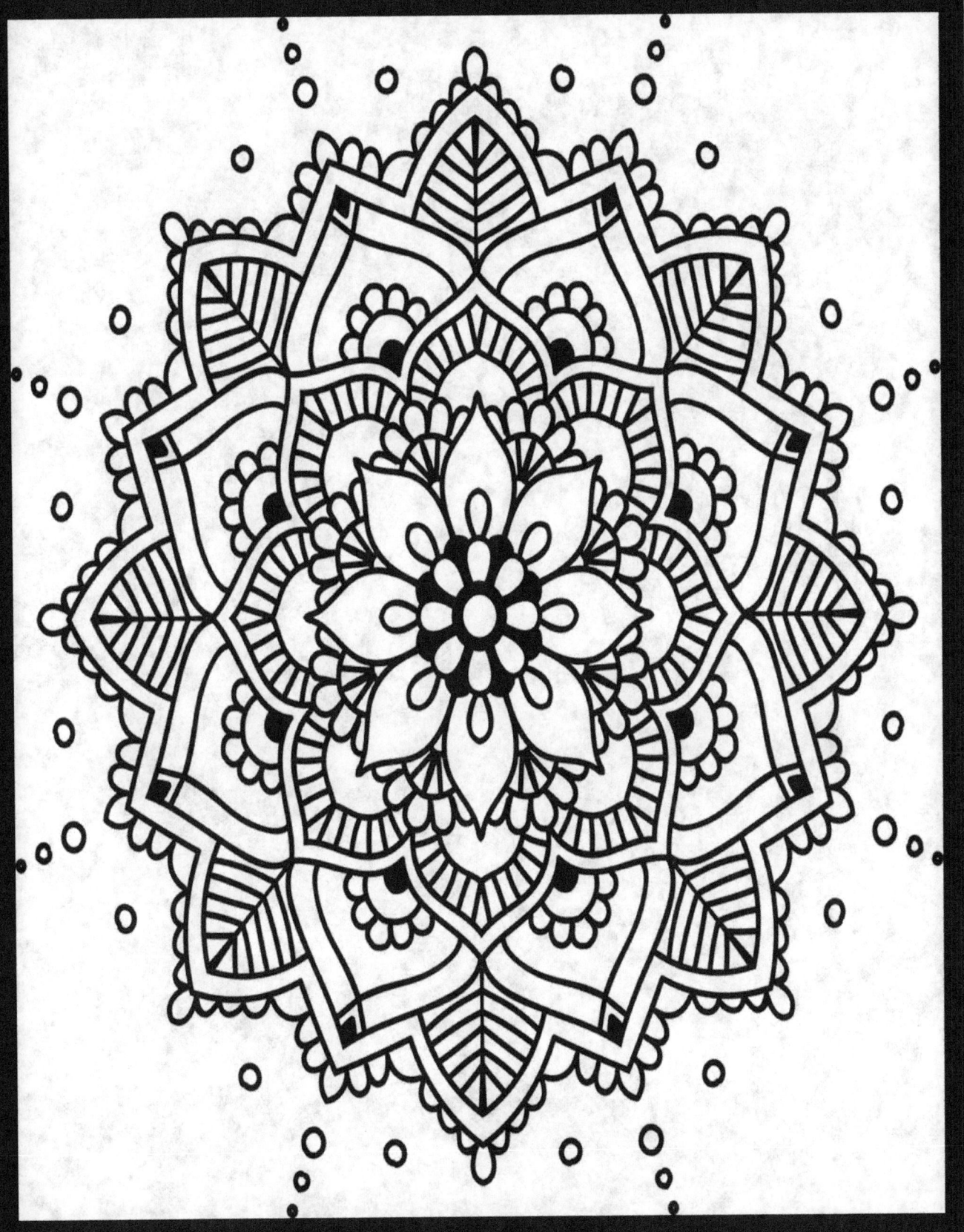

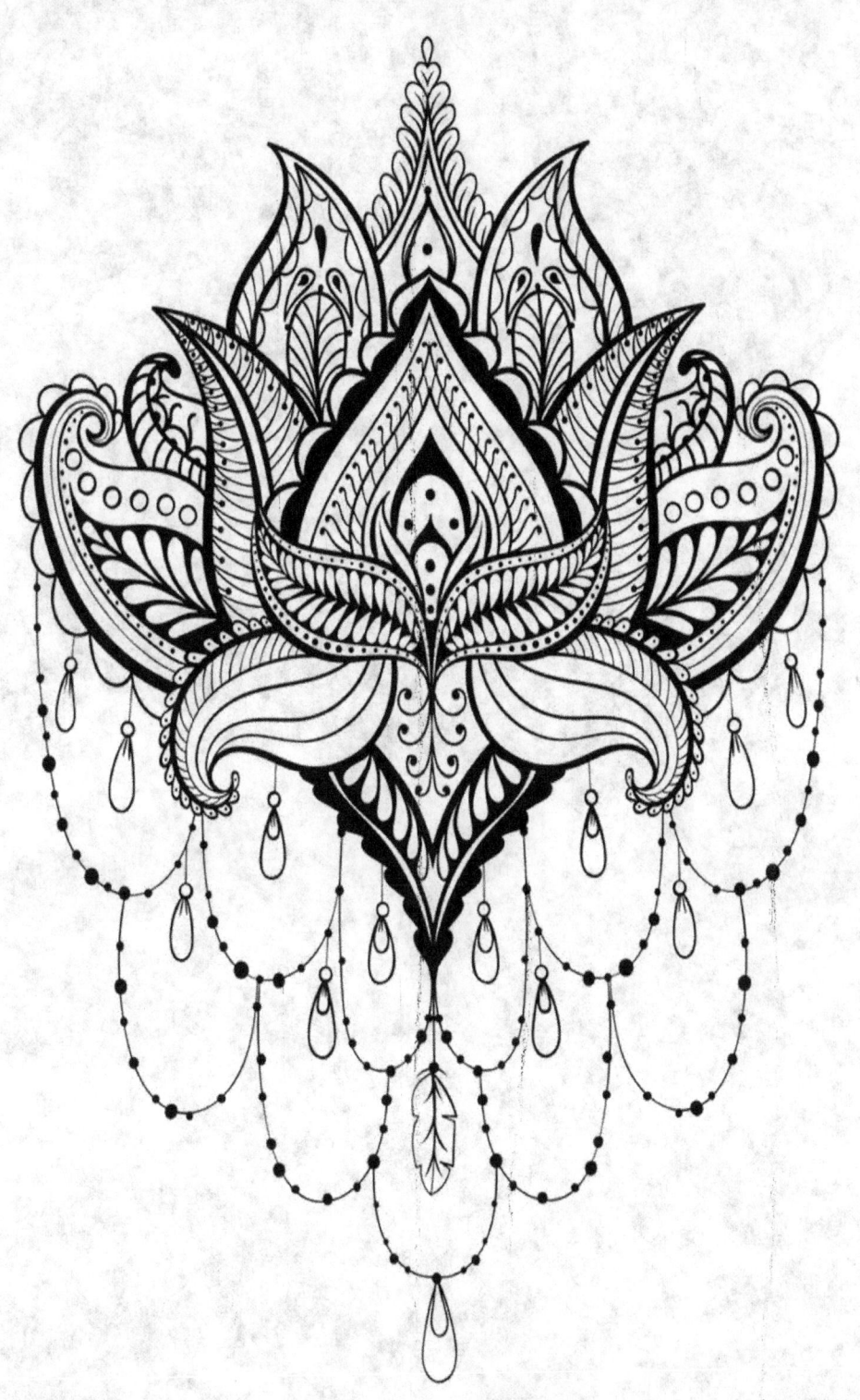

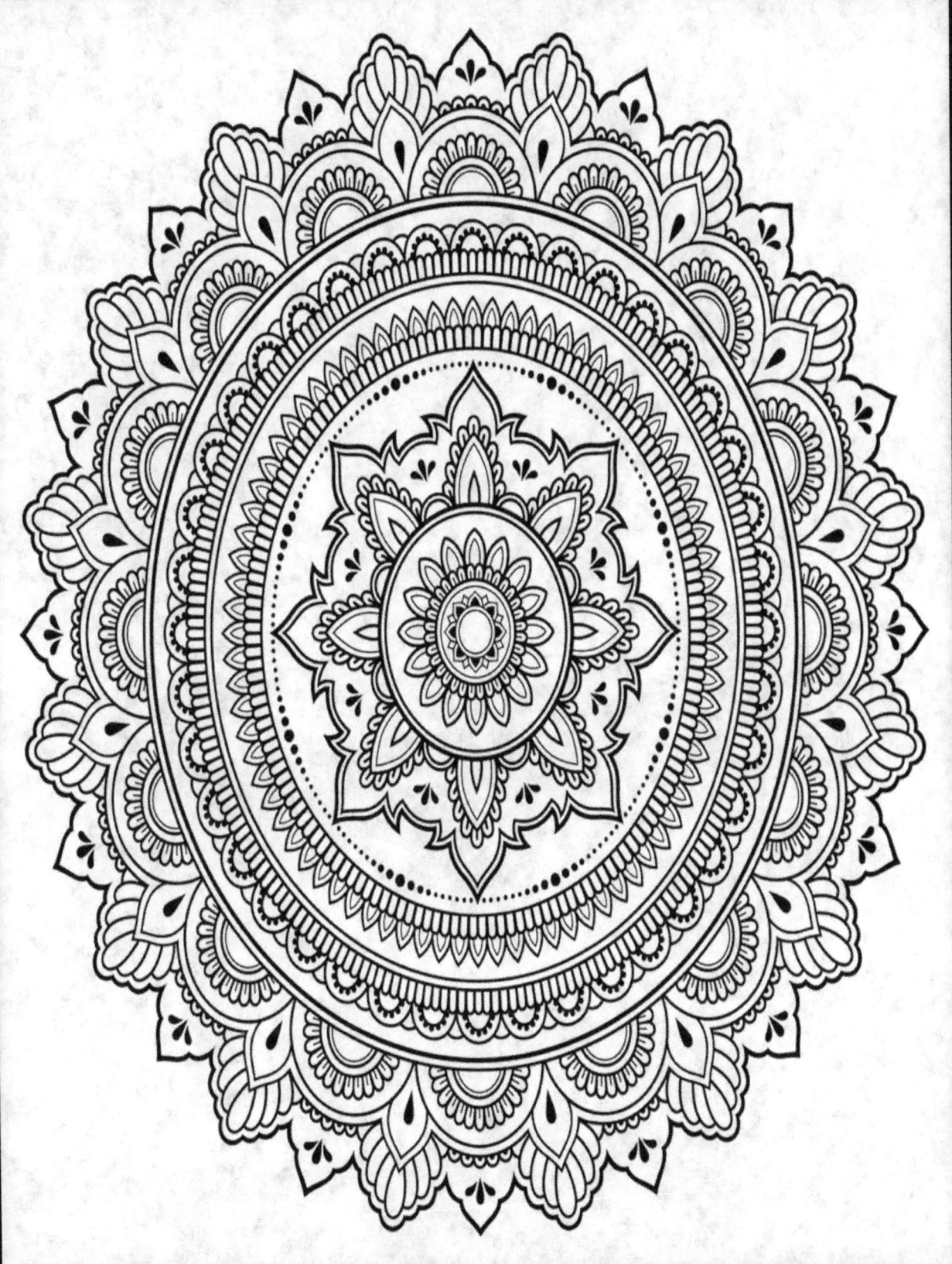

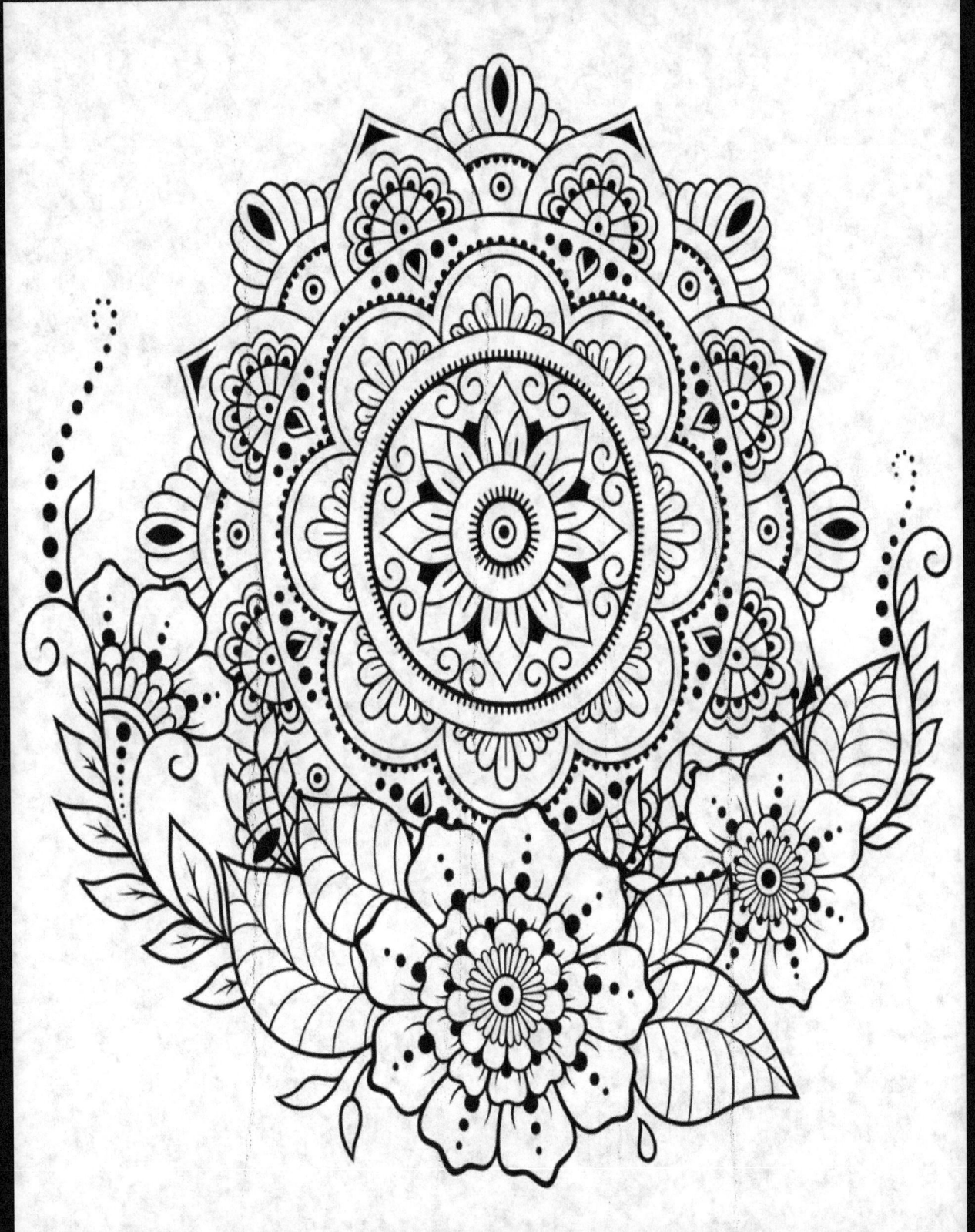

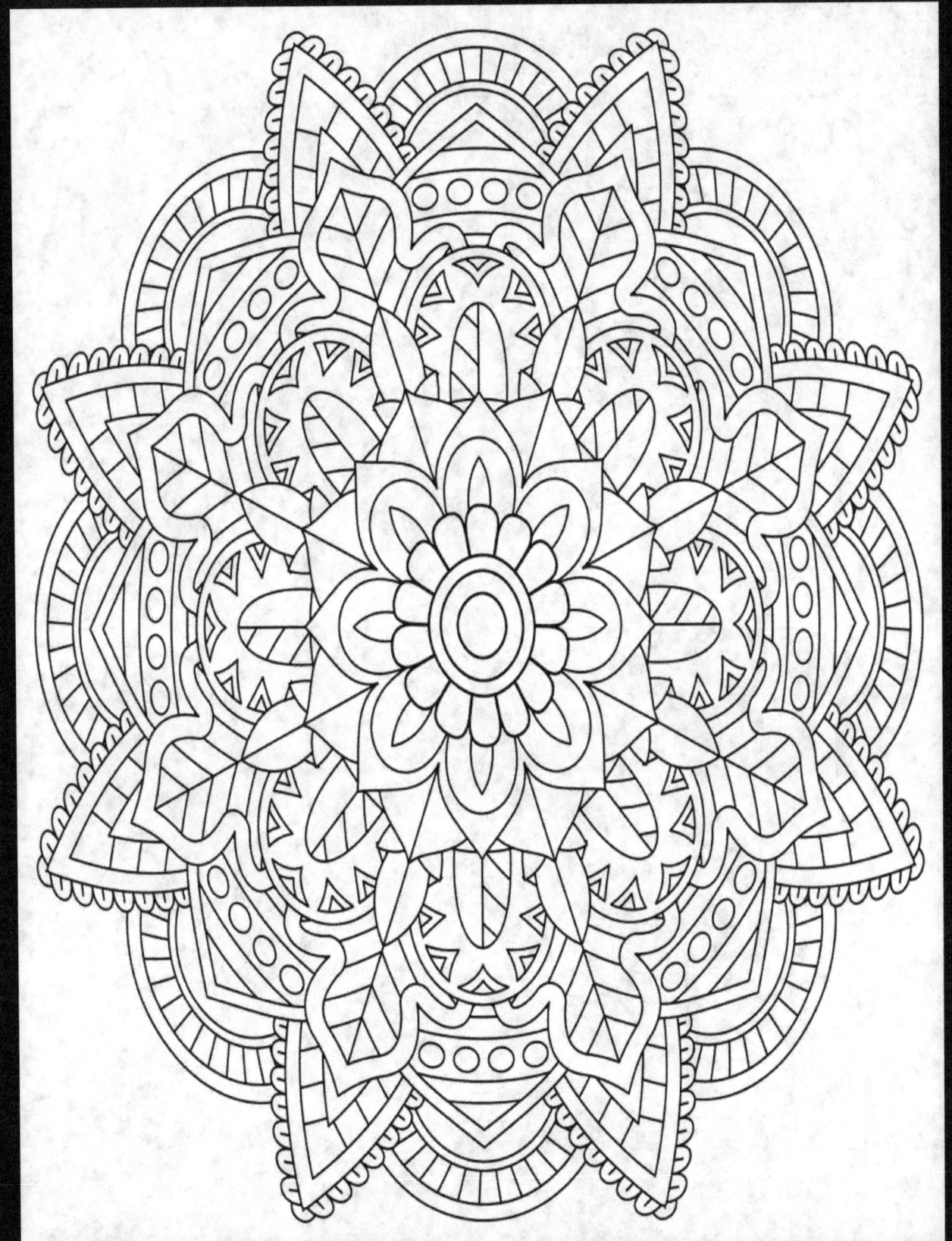

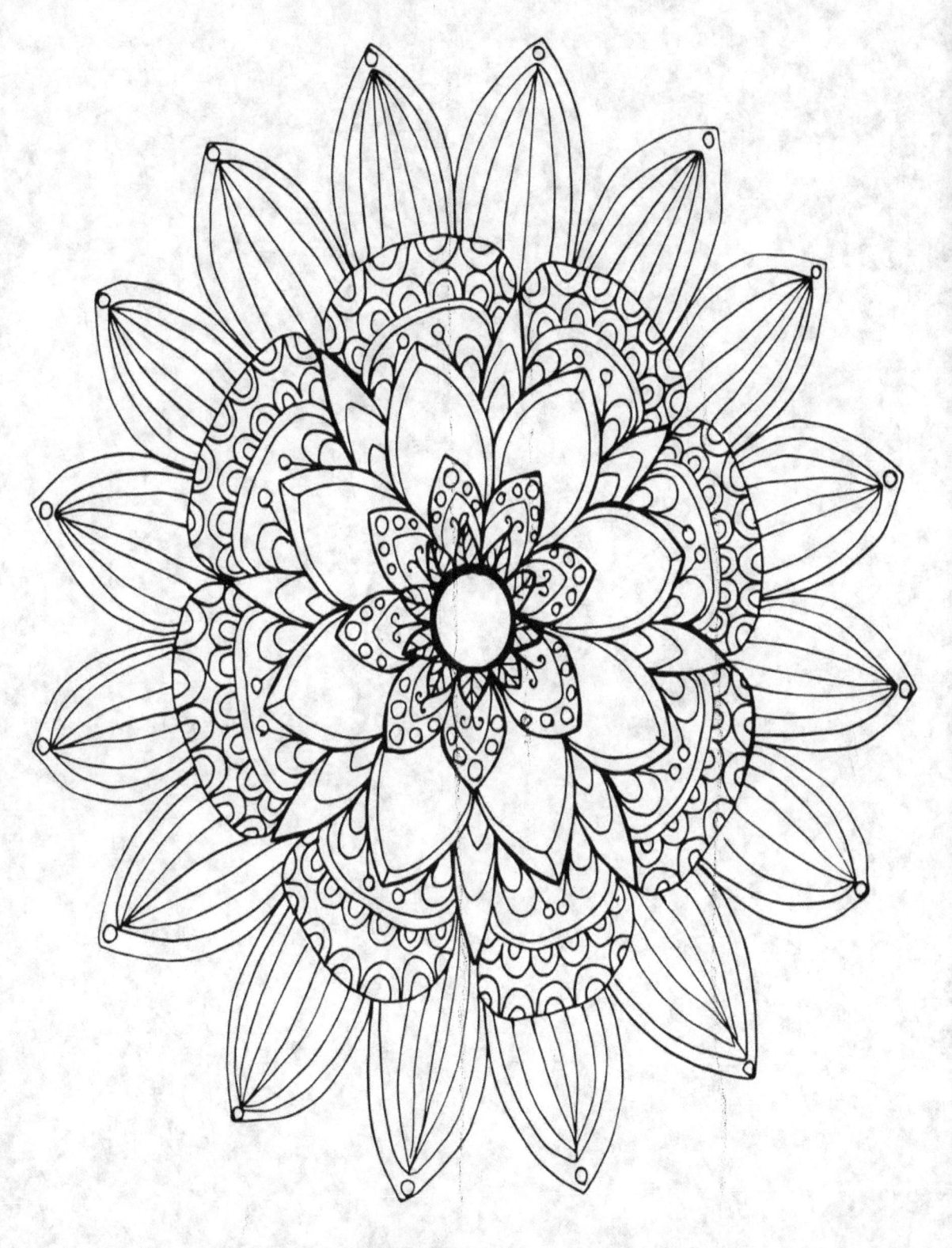

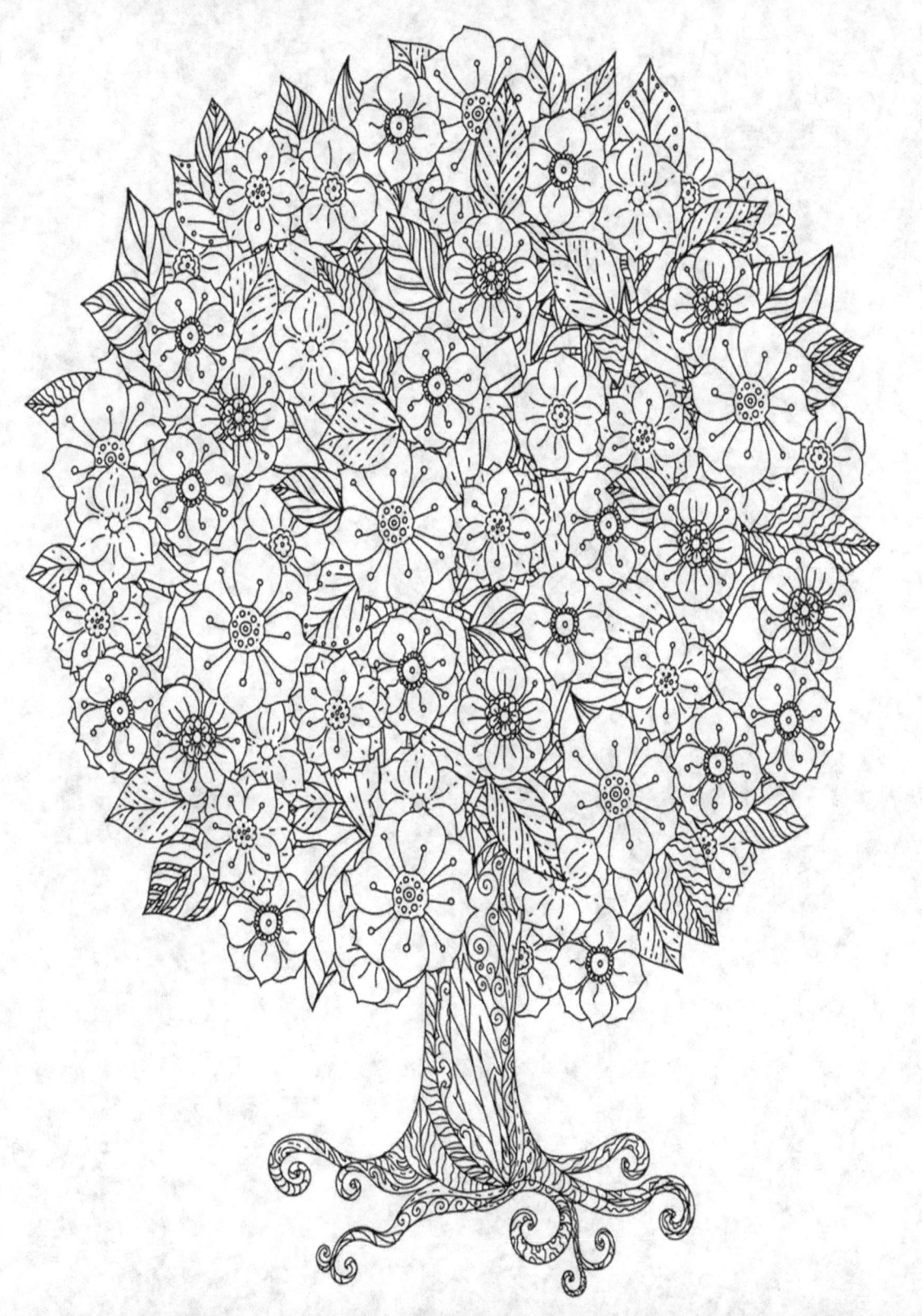

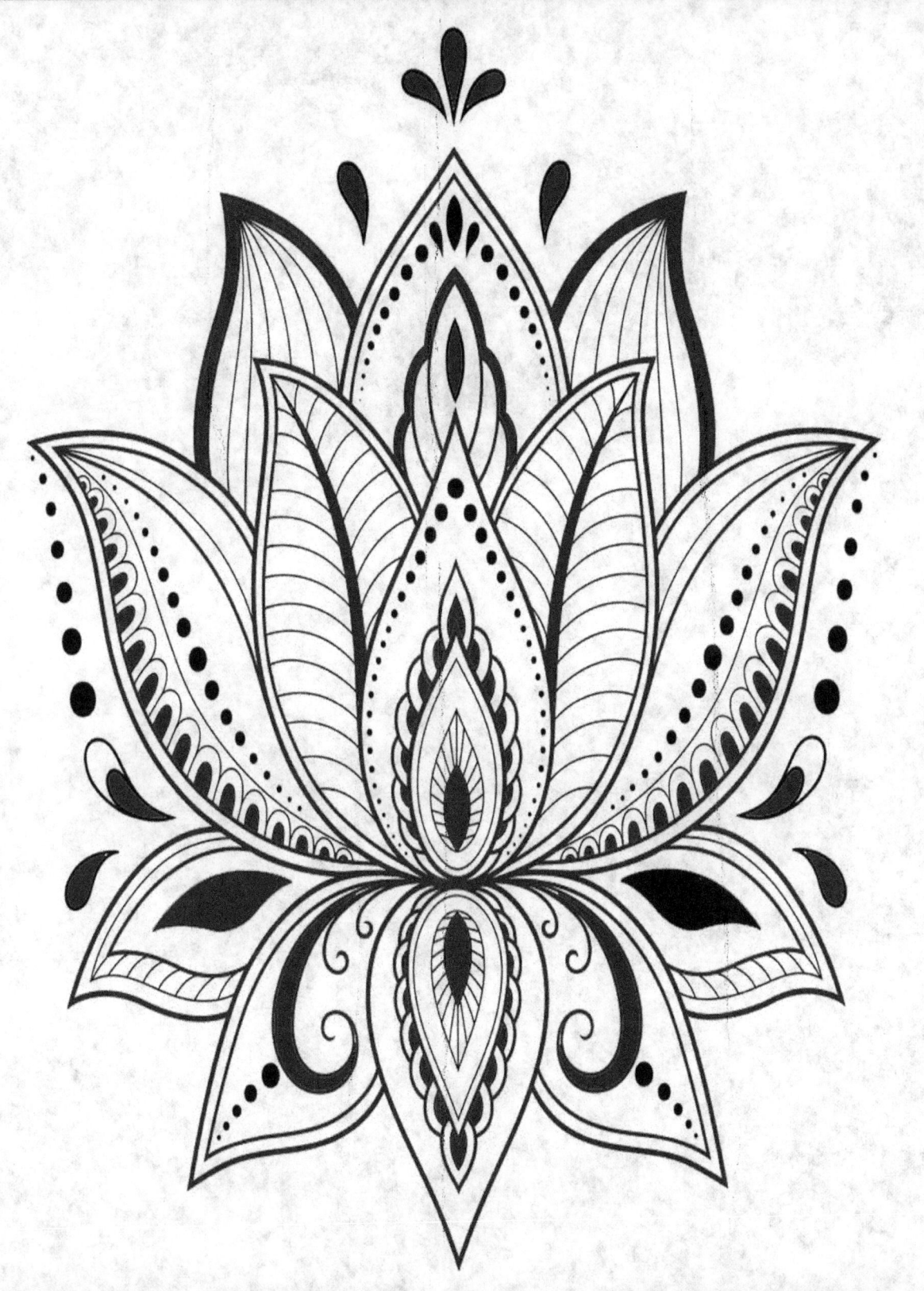

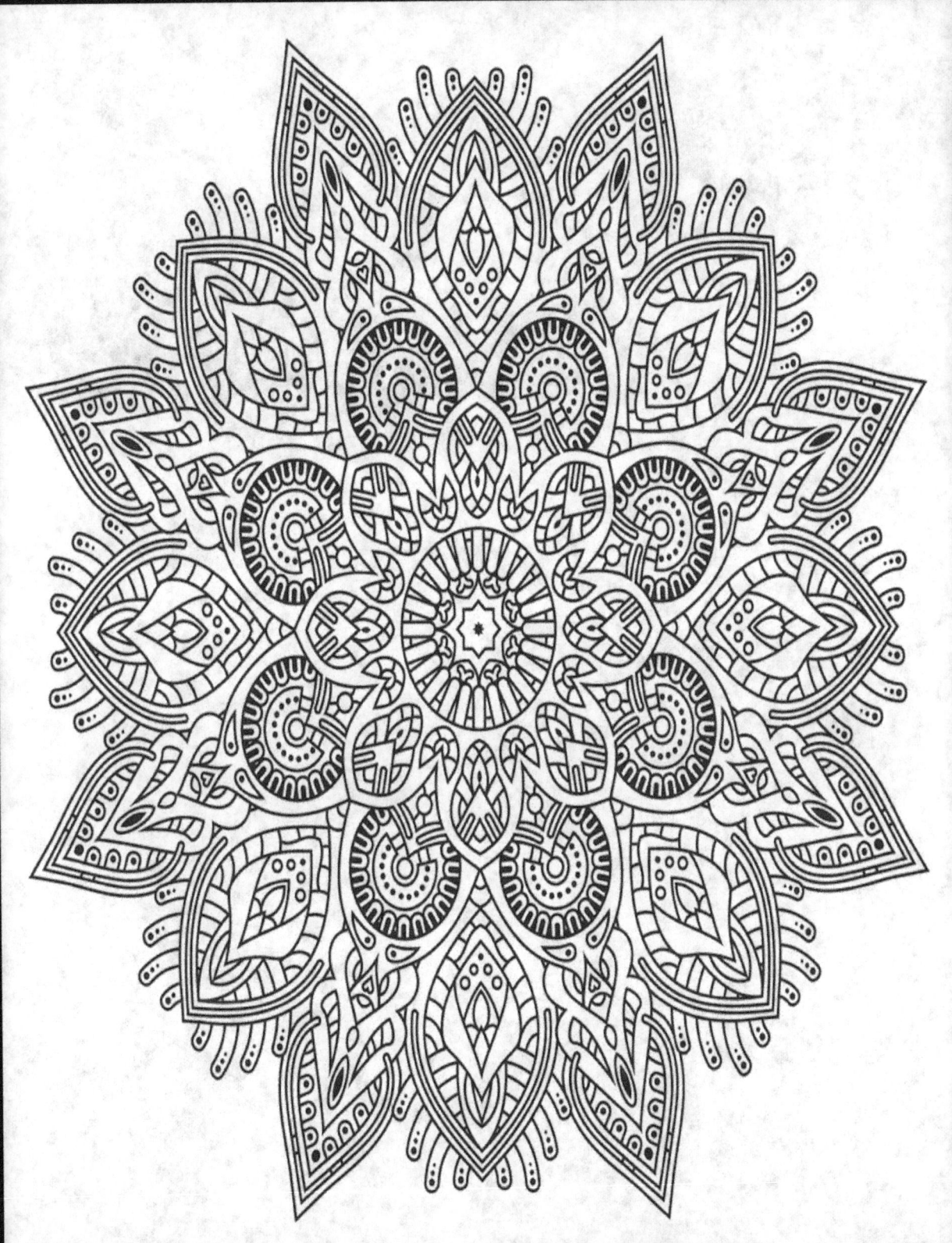

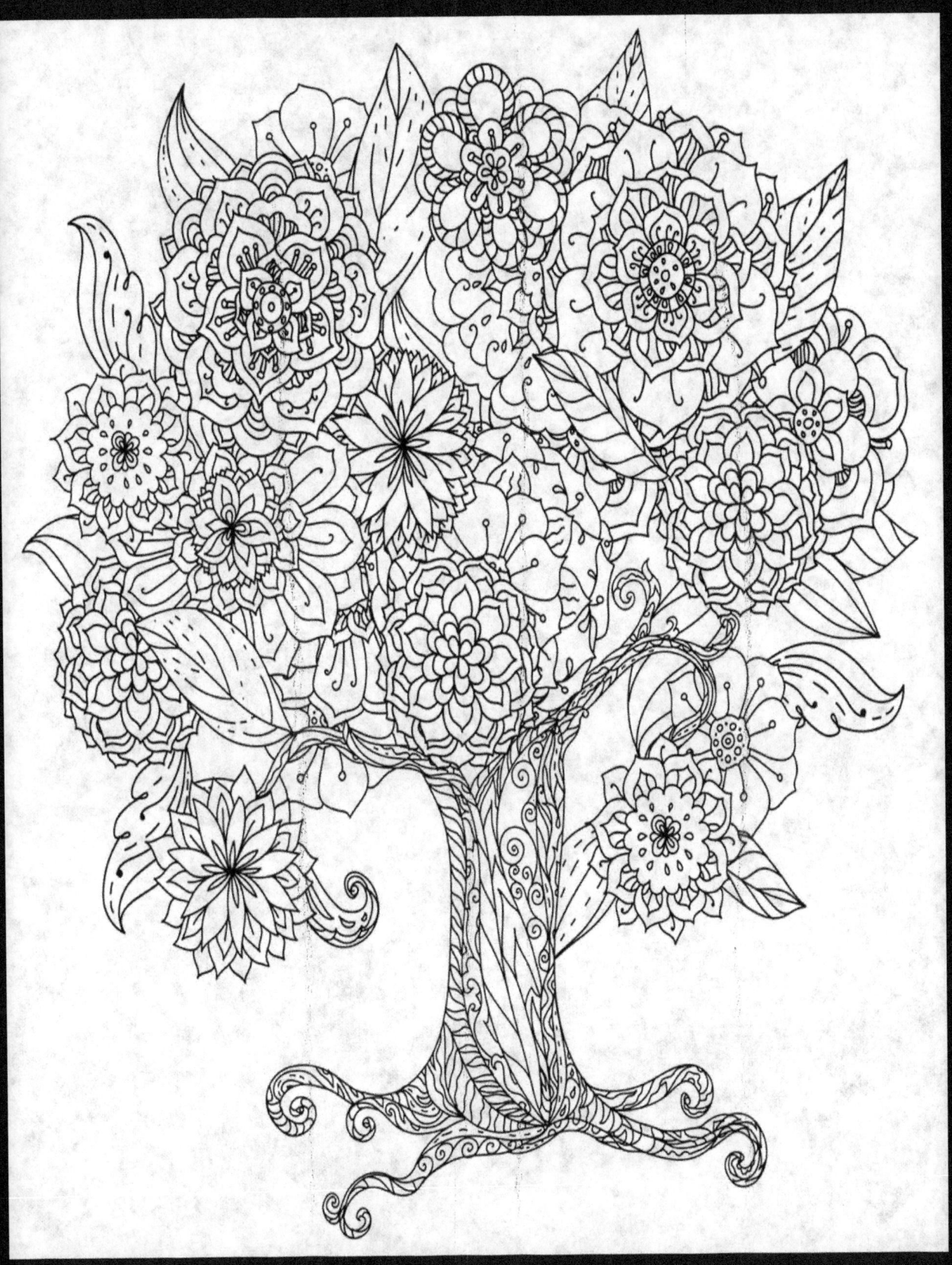

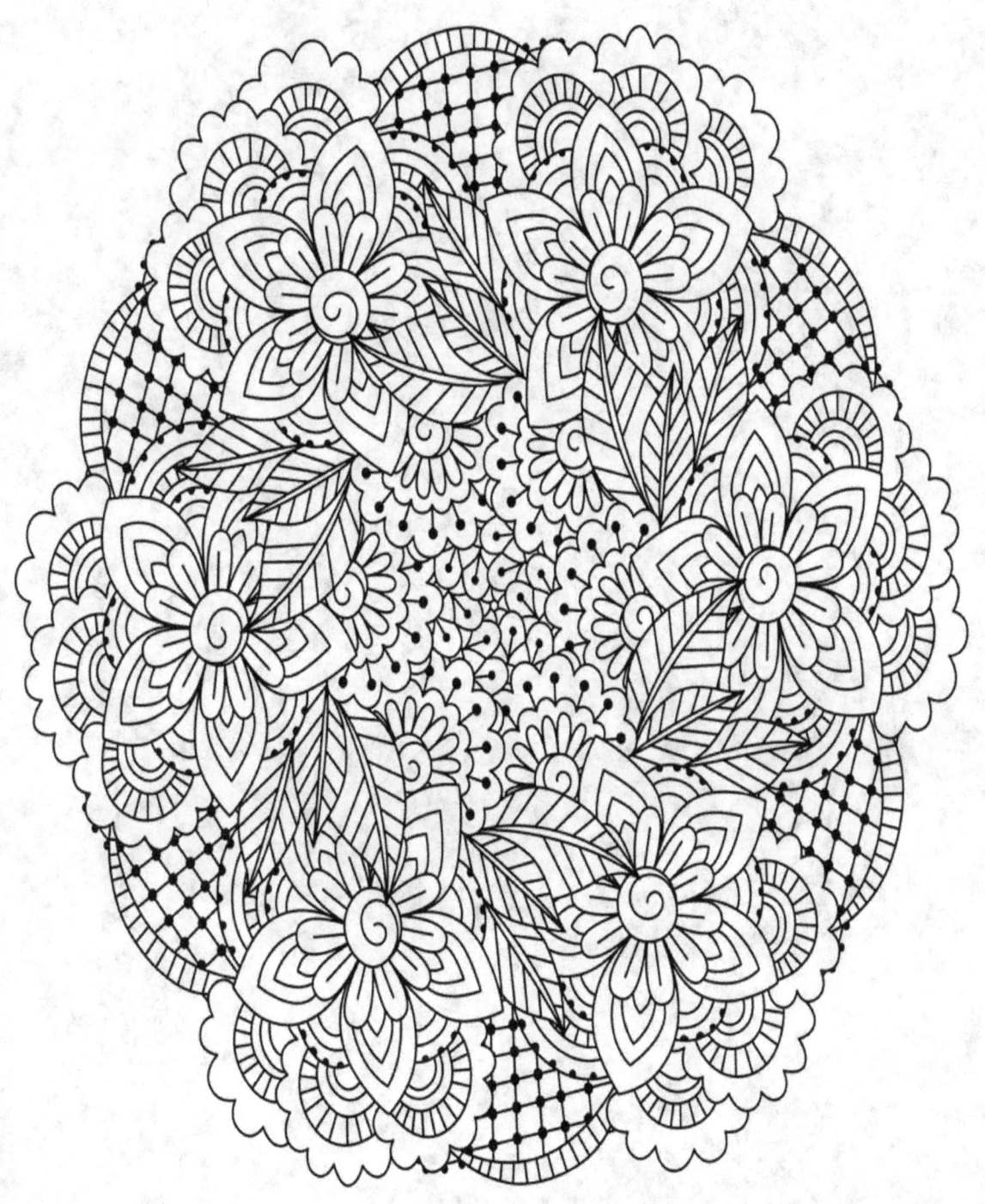

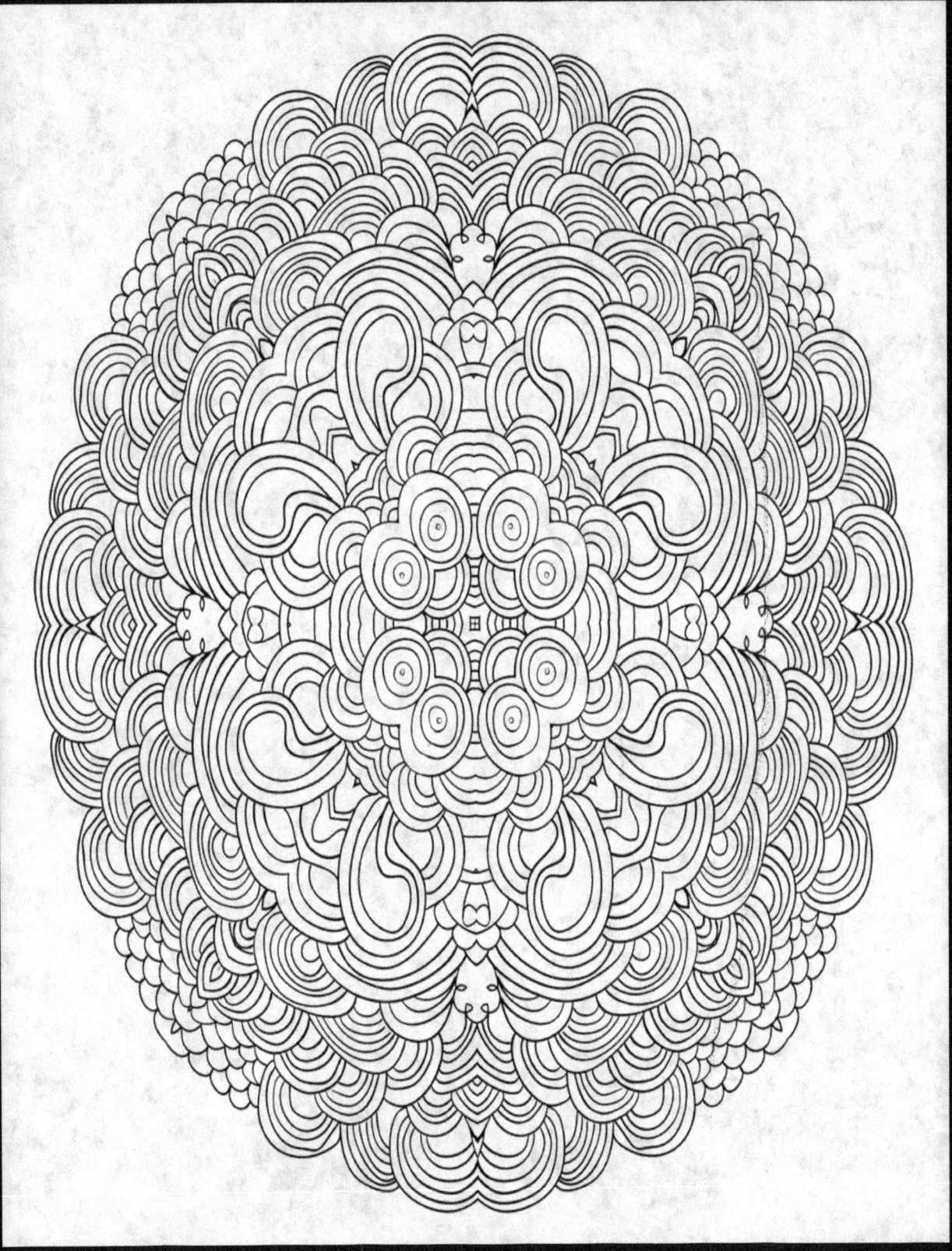

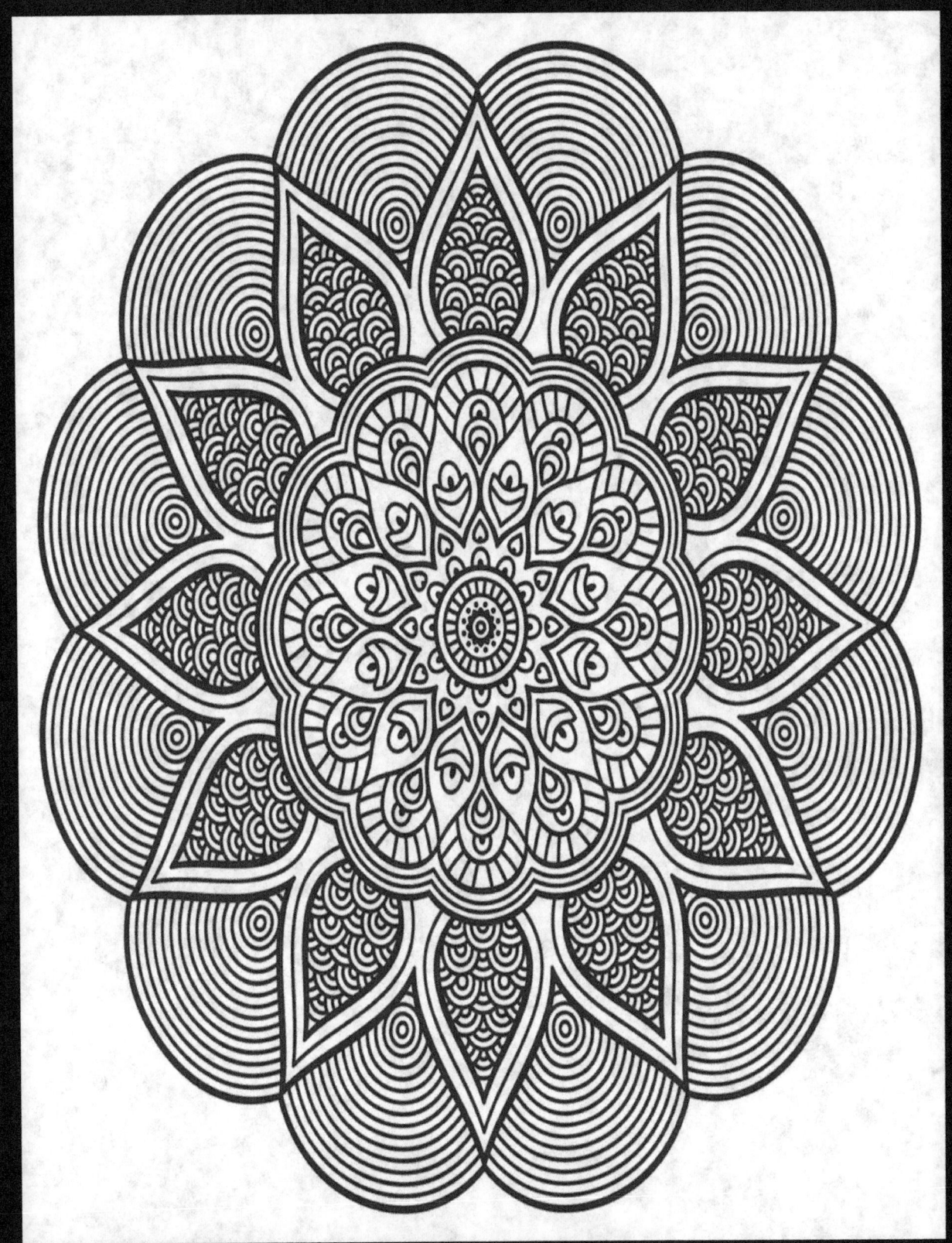

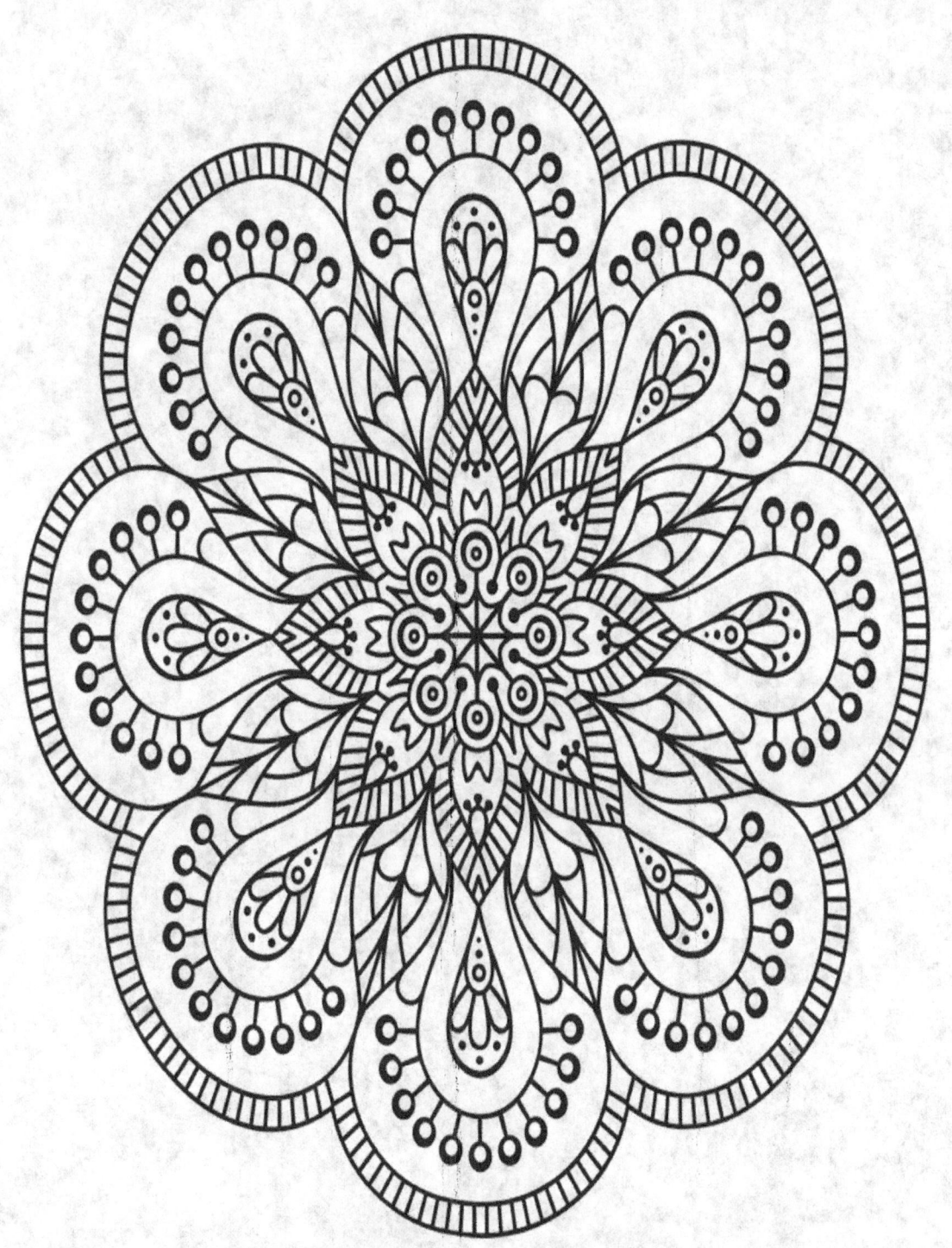

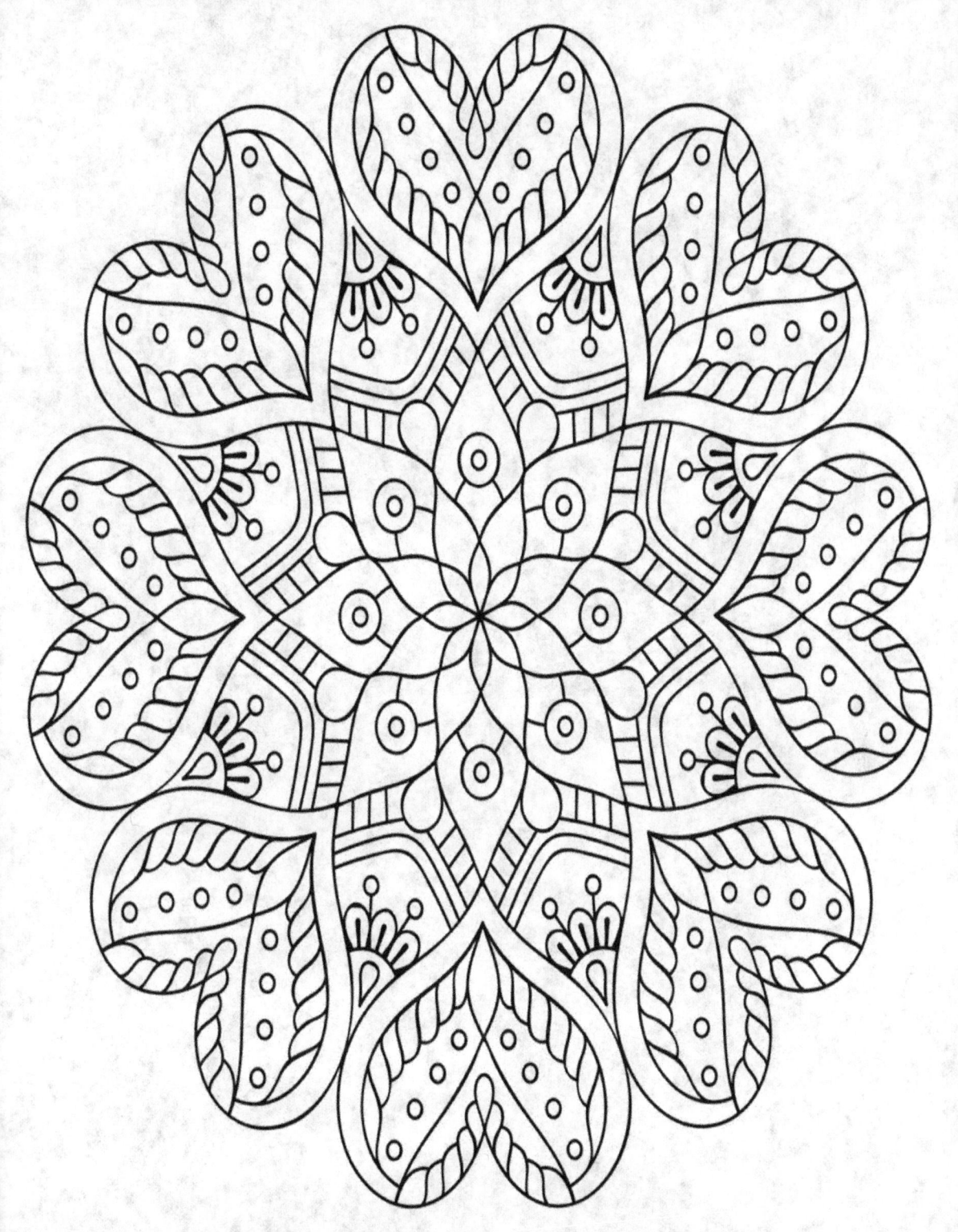

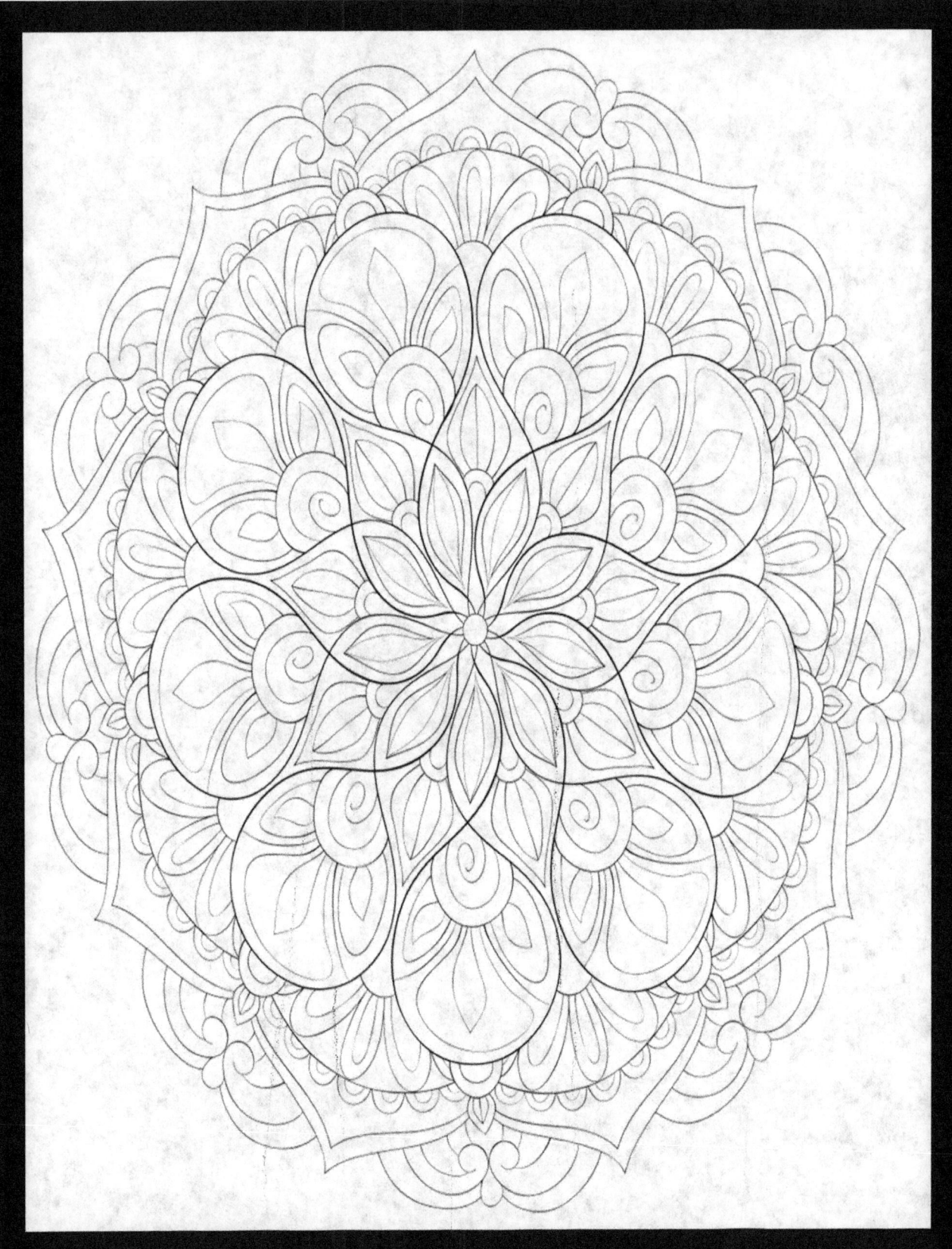

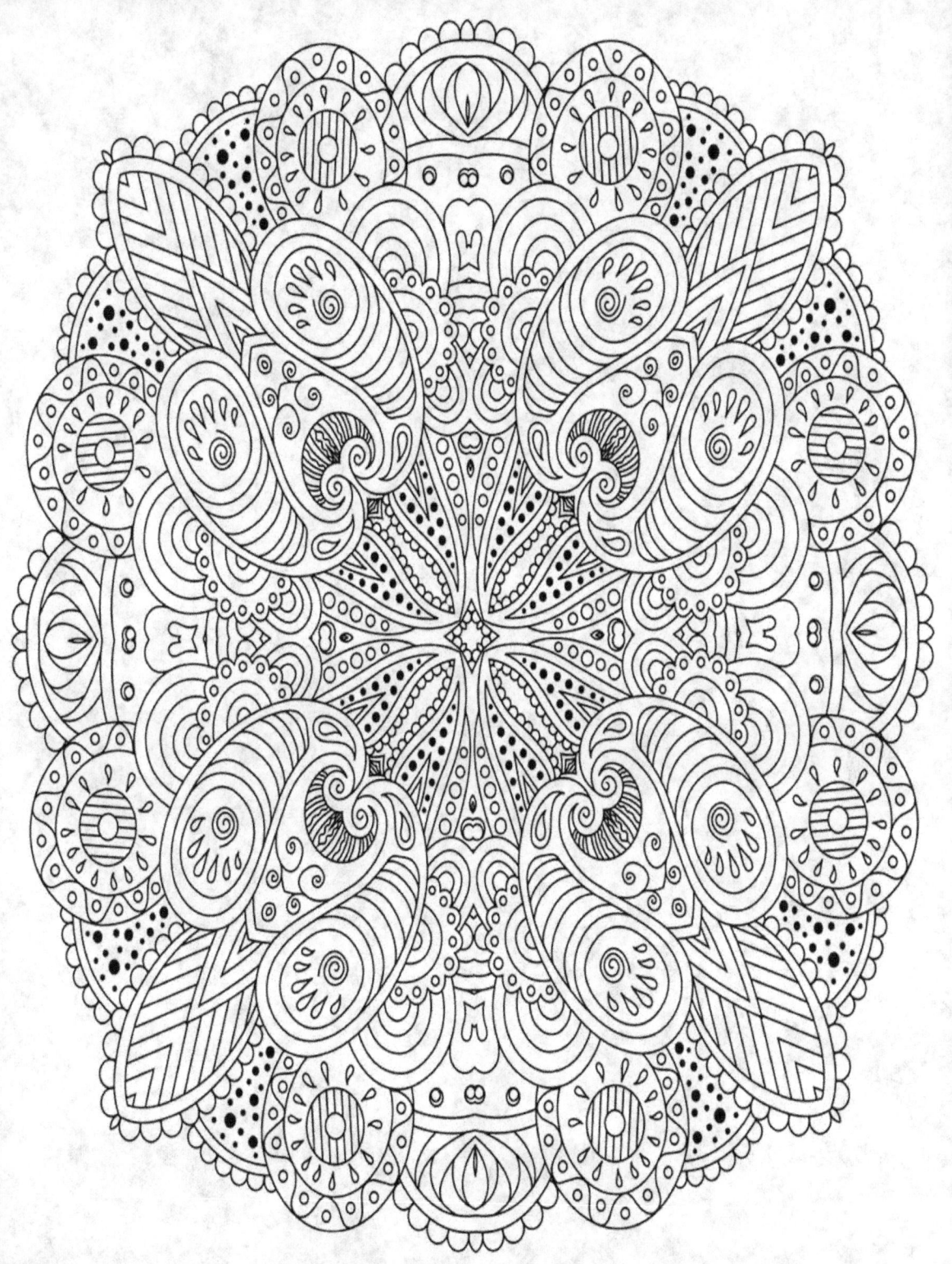

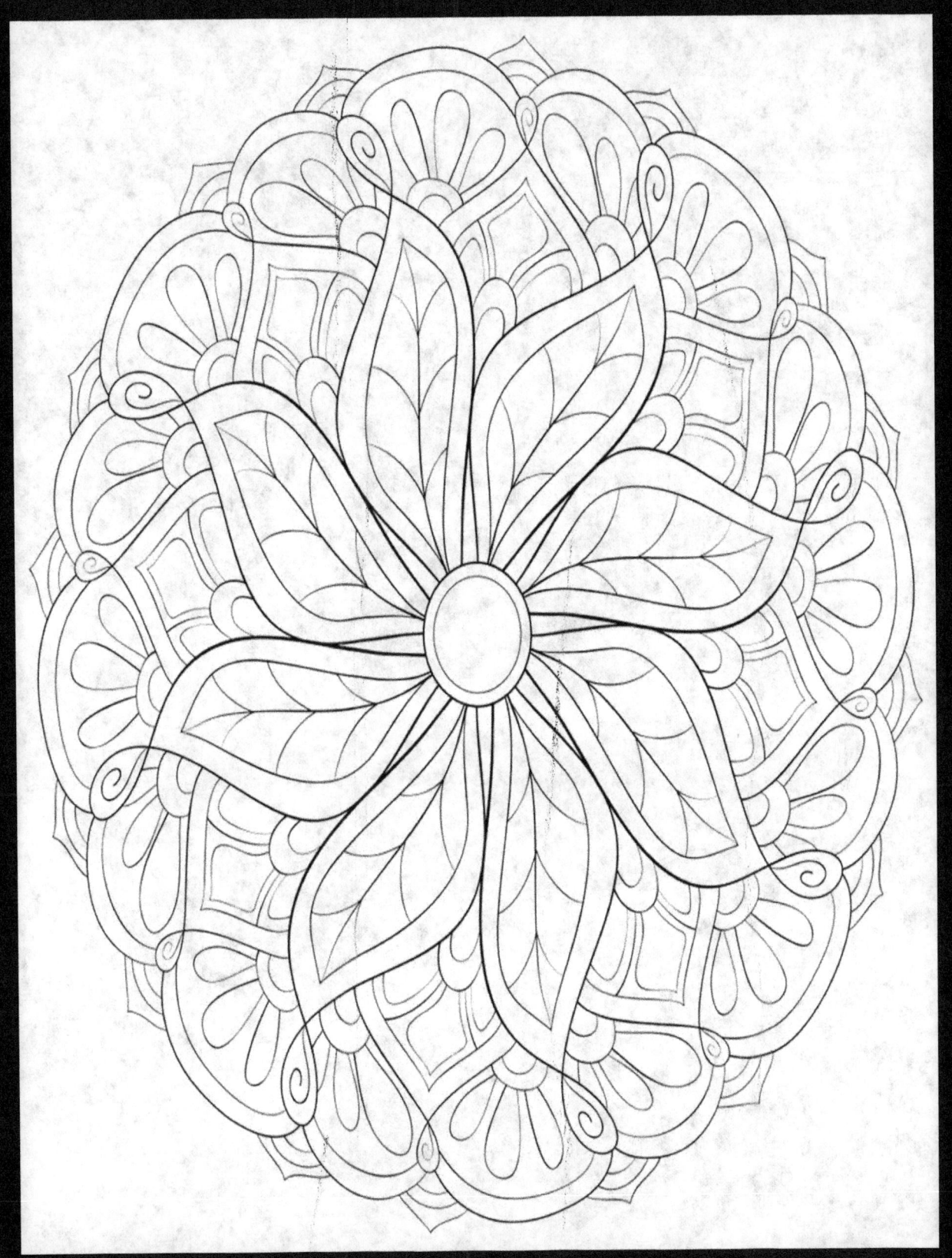

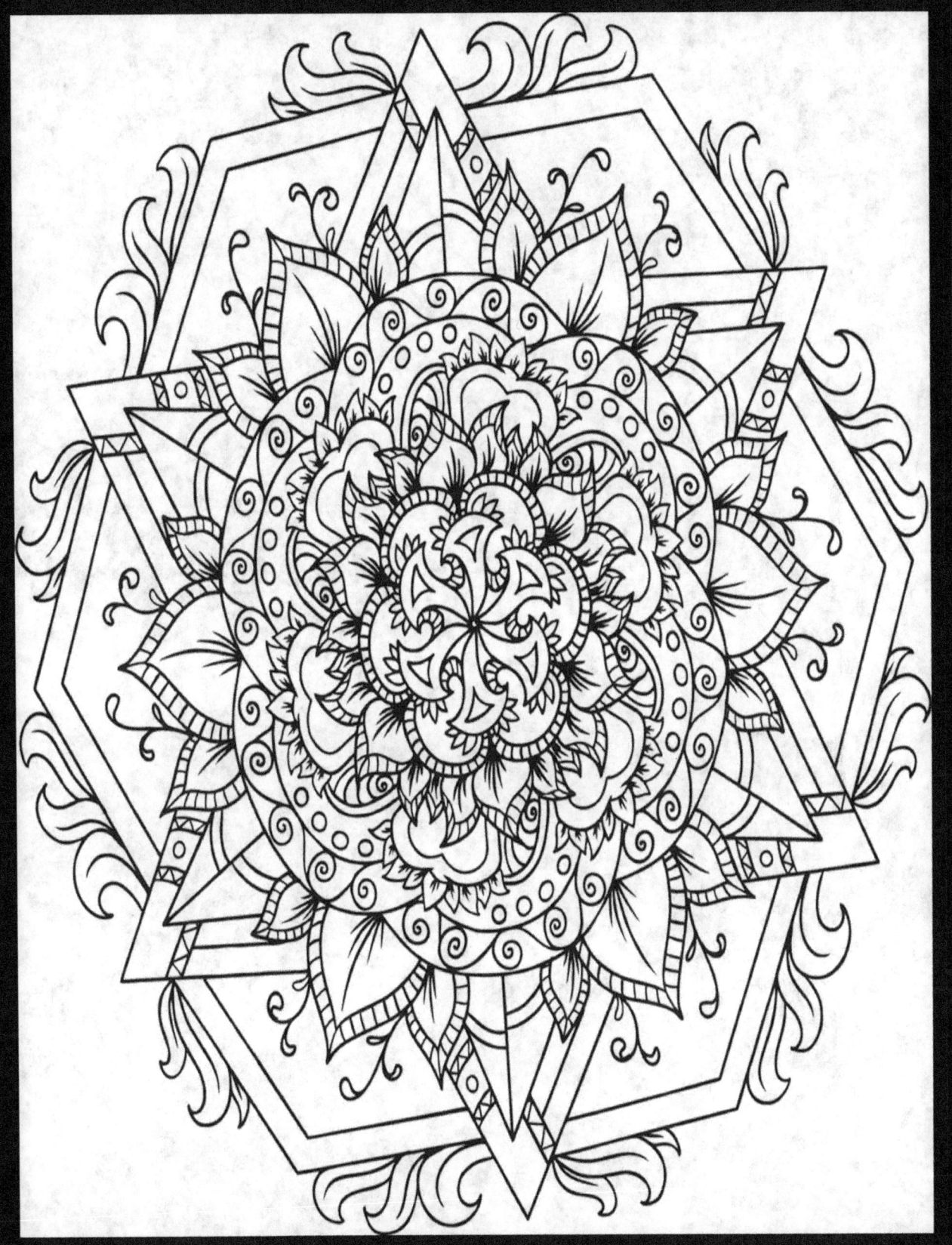

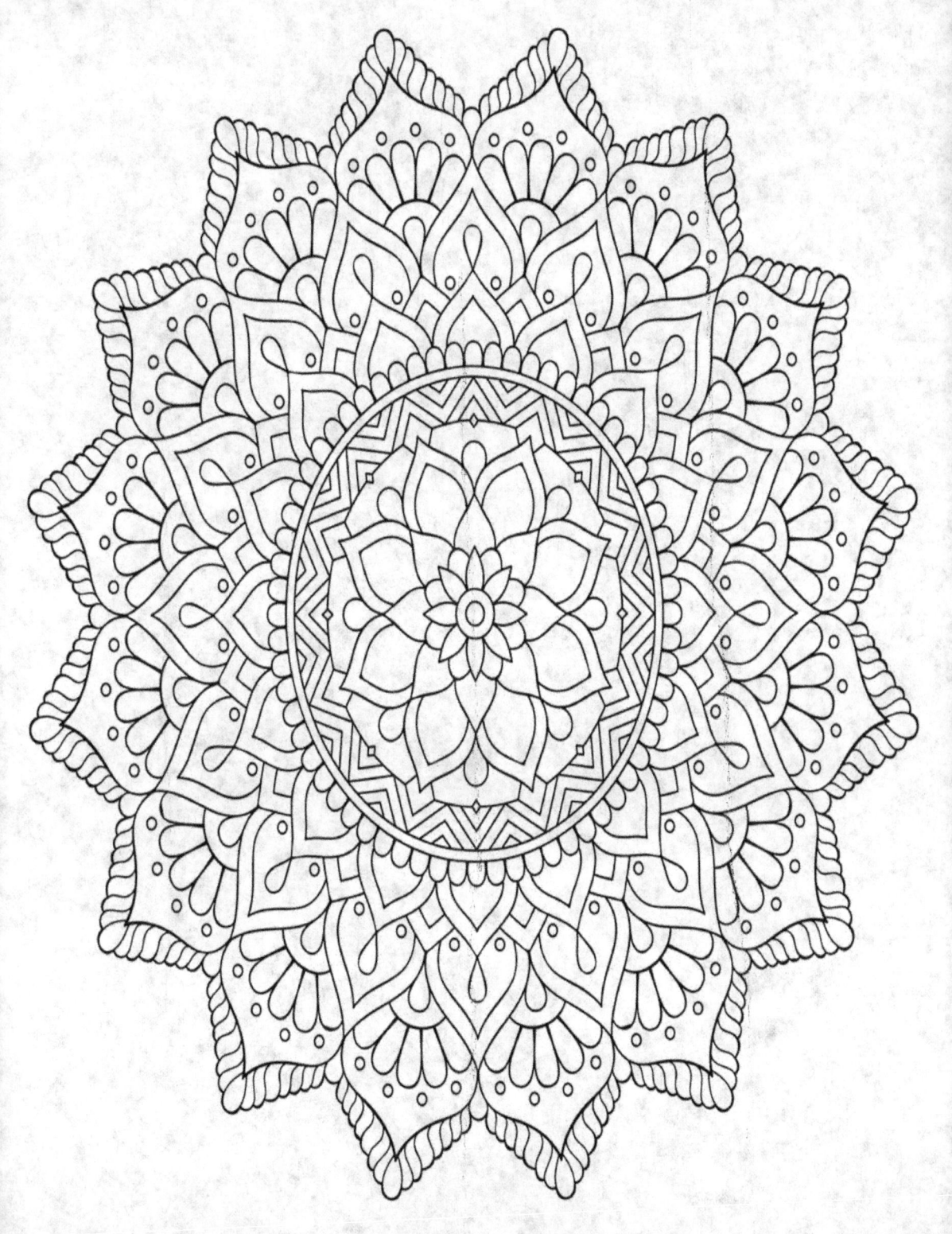

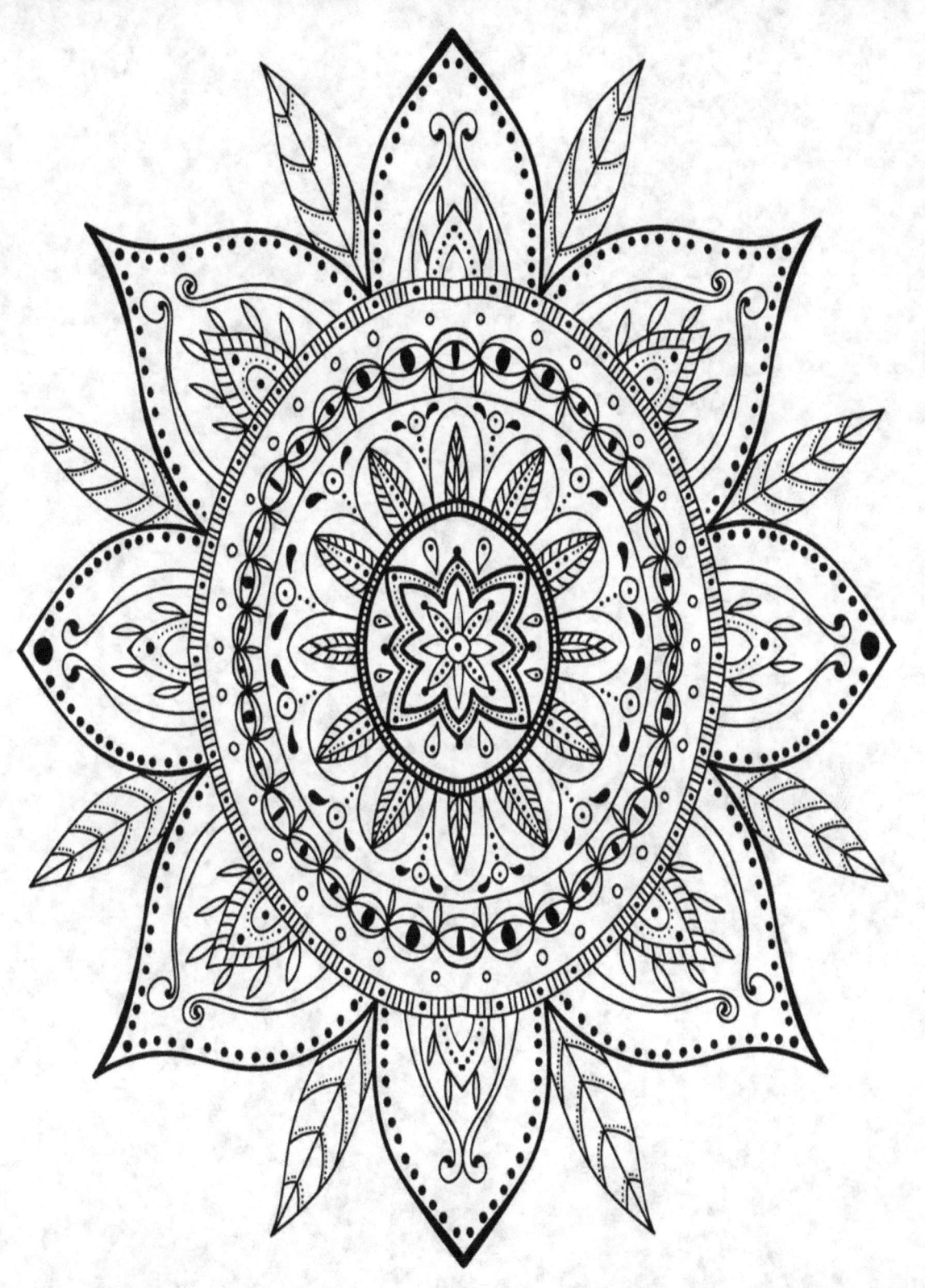

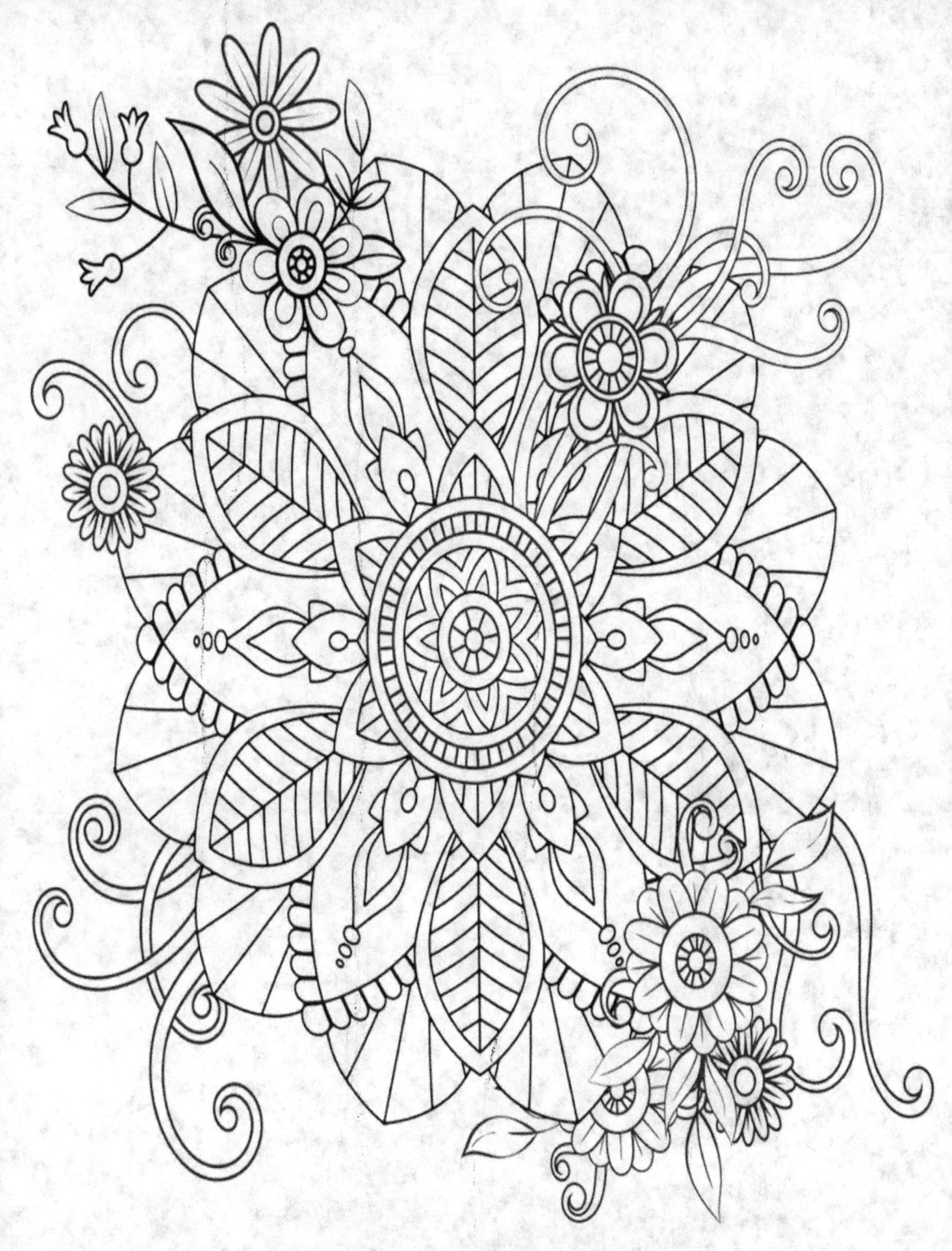

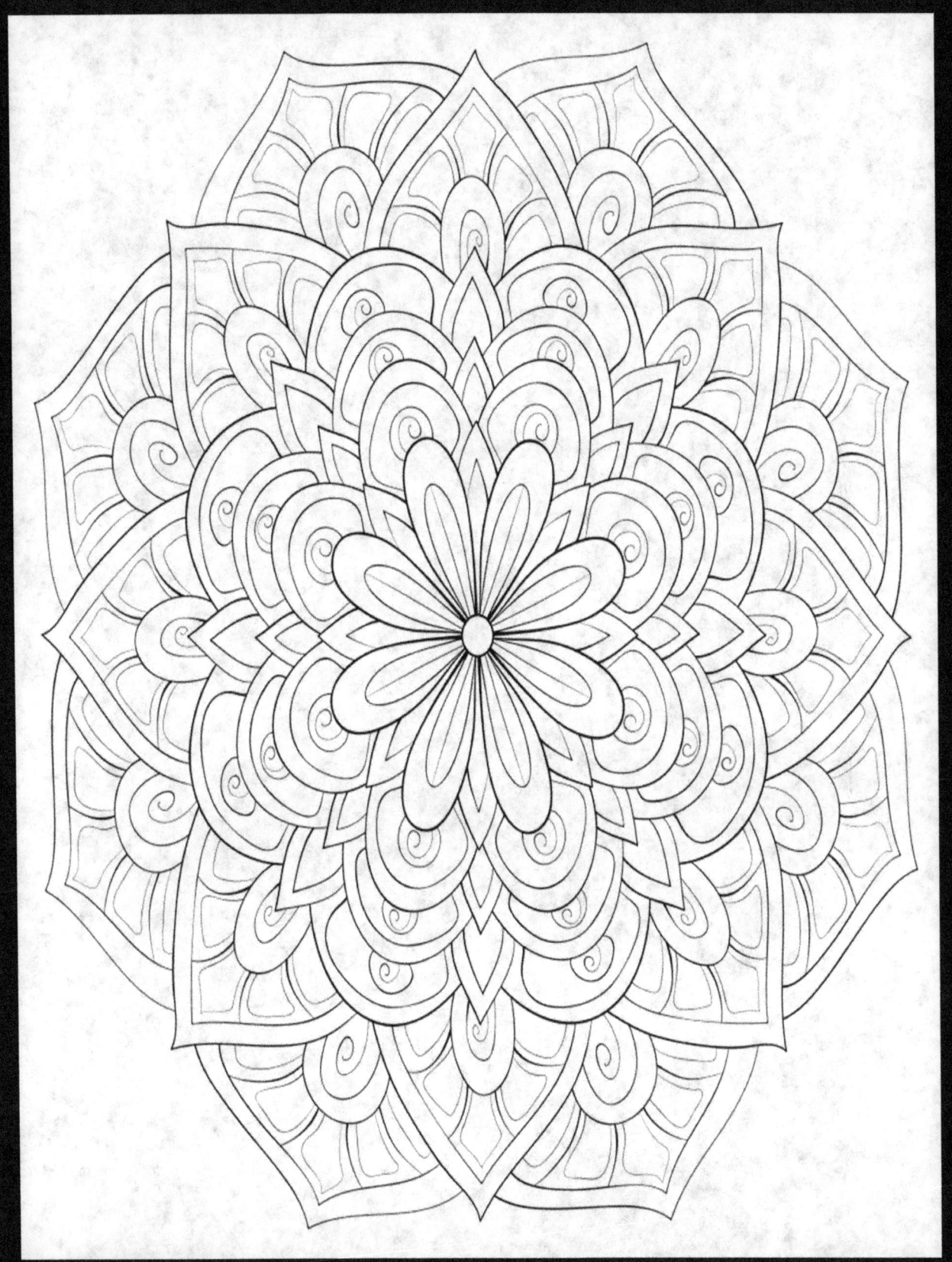

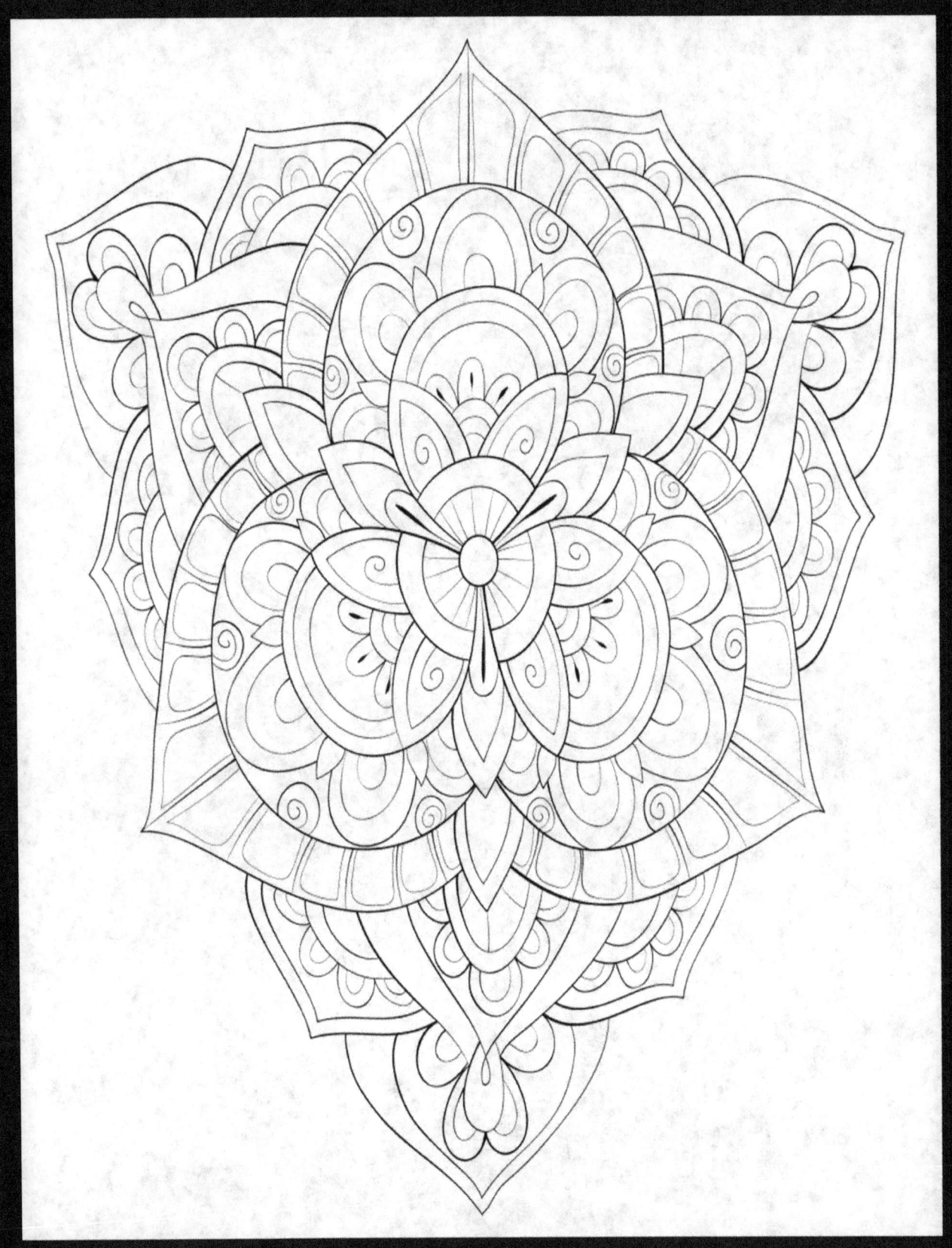

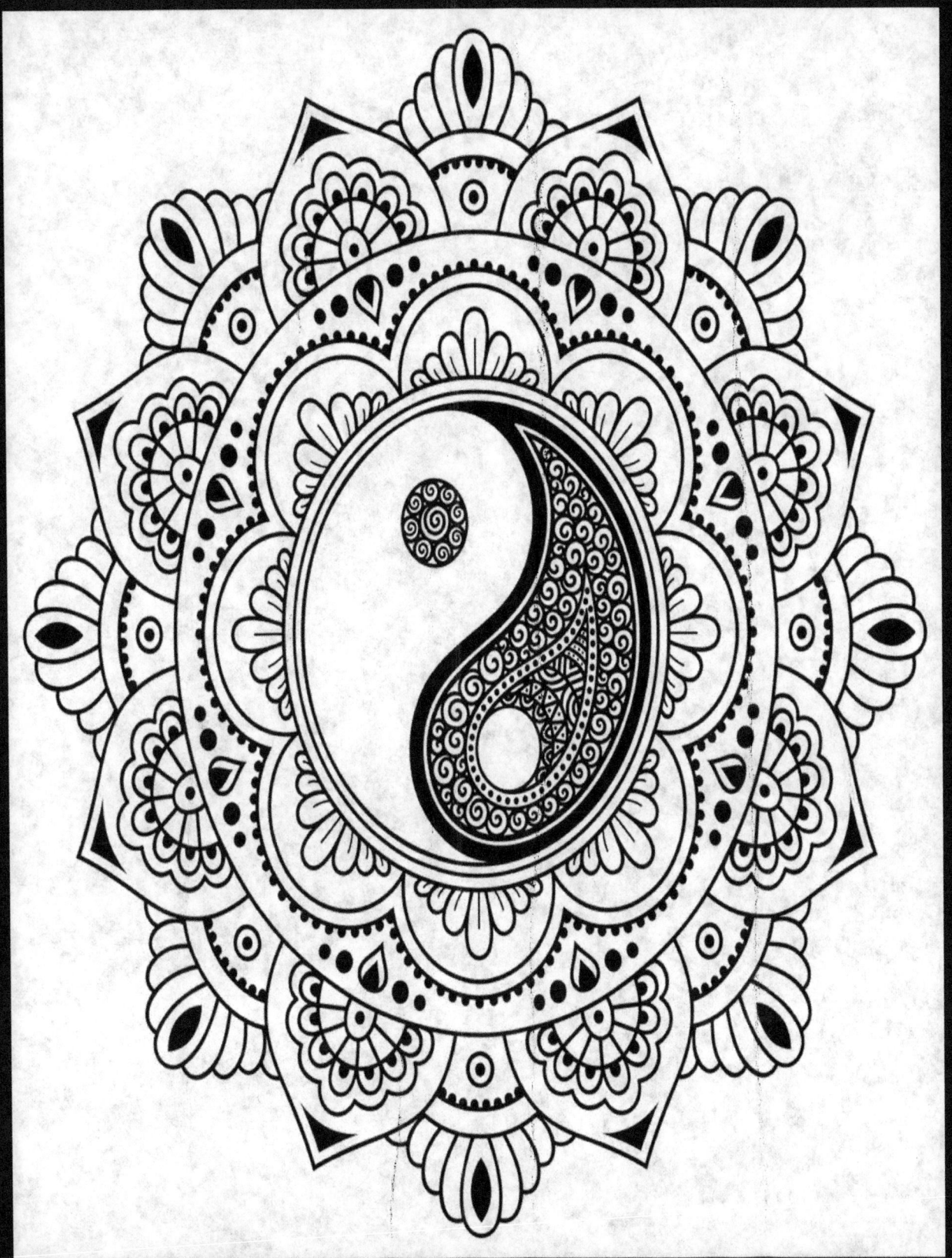

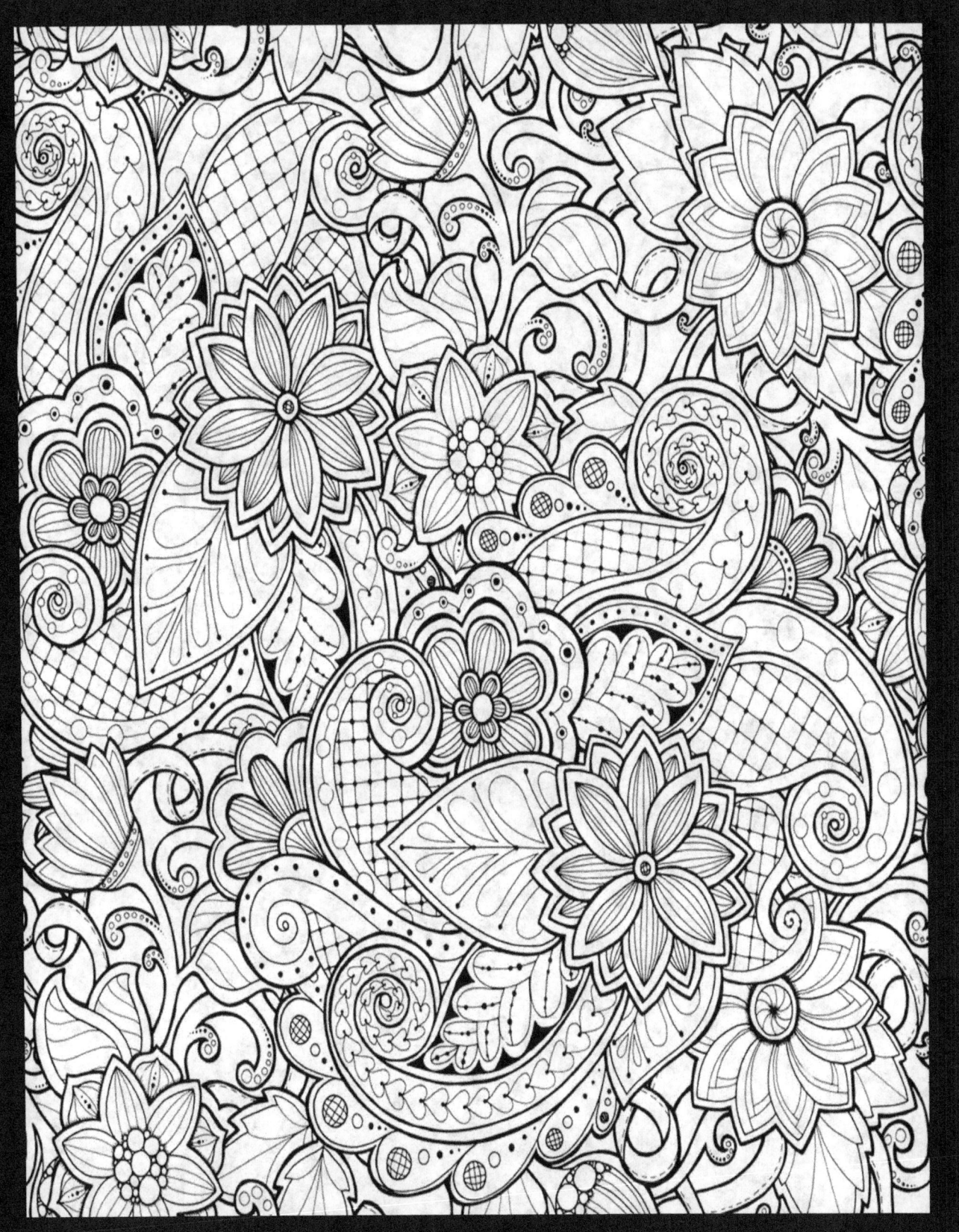

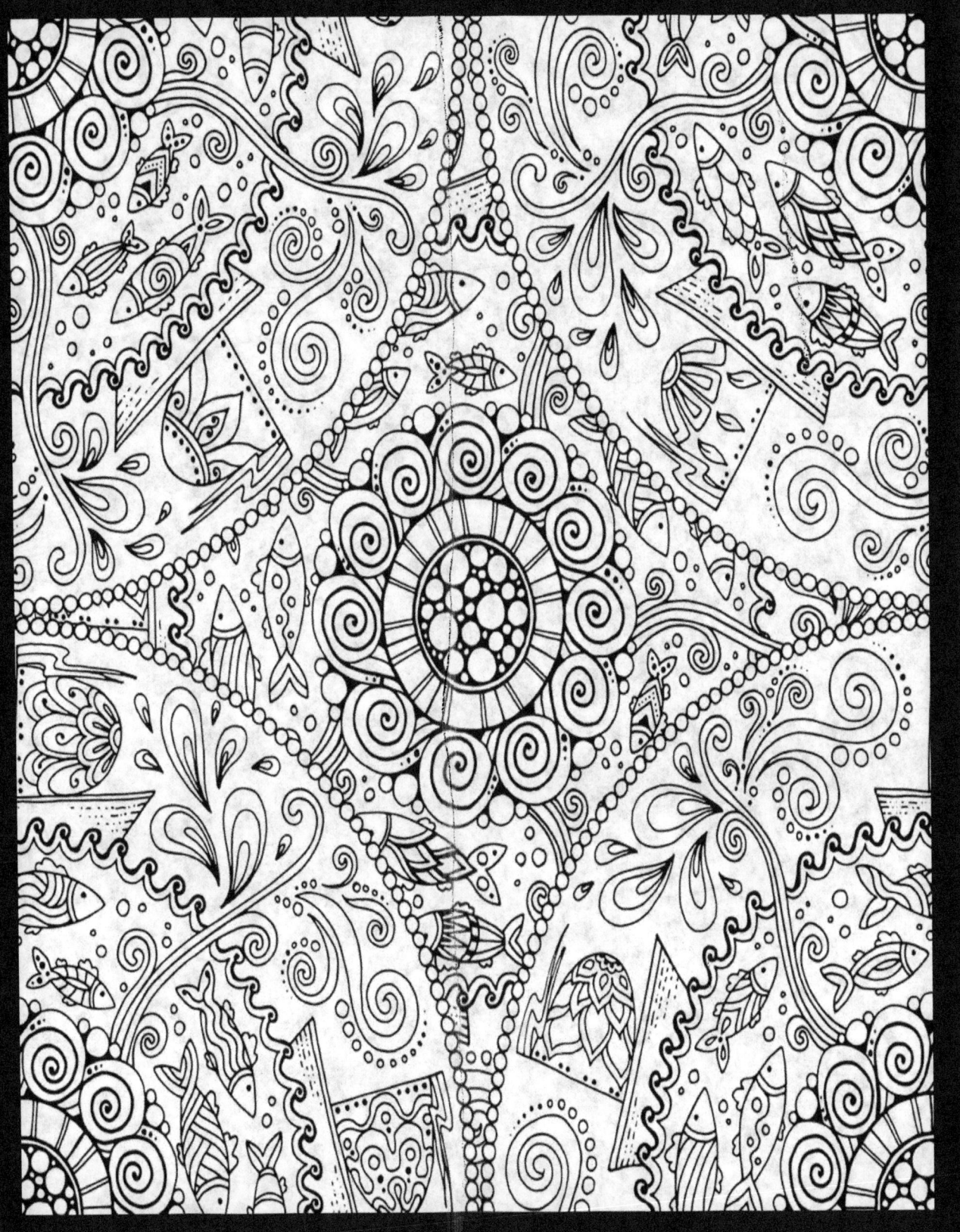

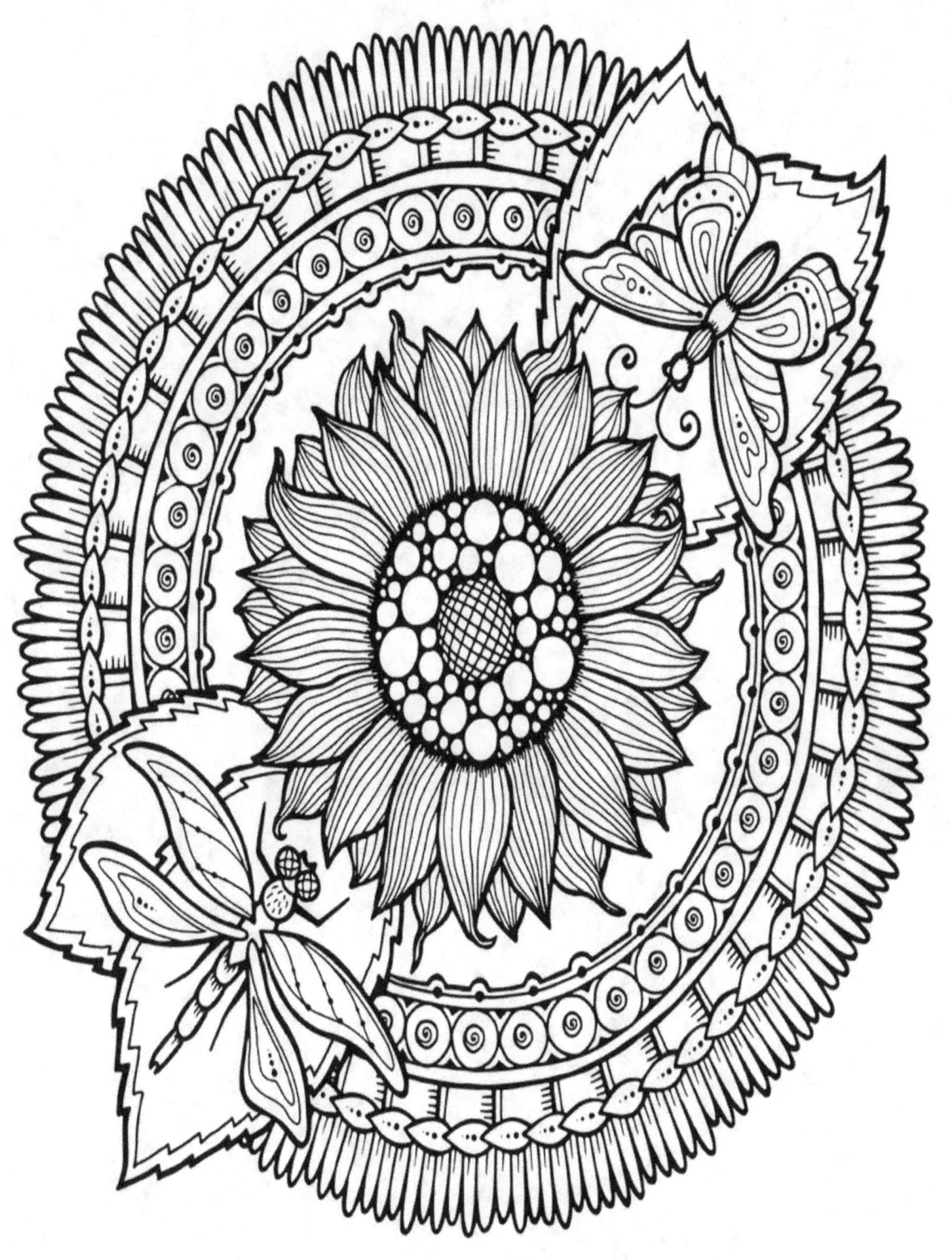

www.ingramcontent.com/pod-product-compliance
Lightning Source LLC
Chambersburg PA
CBHW080505220526
45465CB00006B/2387